LEARNING KOREAN THROUGH TASKS:

HIGH BEGINNER TO LOW INTERMEDIATE

실생활 태스크로 배우는 한국어

YouJin Kim / Bumyong Choi / Hyunae Yun / Binna Kim / Sanghee Kang

KONG & PARK

LEARNING KOREAN THROUGH TASKS: HIGH BEGINNER TO LOW INTERMEDIATE
실생활 태스크로 배우는 한국어

Written by YouJin Kim, Bumyong Choi, Hyunae Yun, Binna Kim, and Sanghee Kang
Edited by Yejoo Lee
Designed by Jong Woo Lee

Published by KONG & PARK USA, INC.
1440 Renaissance Drive, Suite 430
Park Ridge, IL 60068 USA
Tel +1 (847) 241 4845
Fax +1 (312) 757 5553
usaoffice@kongnpark.com
www.kongnpark.com

1st published January 25, 2021

ISBN 9781635190250

Library of Congress Control Number: 2021930113

DISTRIBUTORS

United States: KONG & PARK USA, INC.
1440 Renaissance Drive, Suite 430
Park Ridge, IL 60068
Tel +1 (847) 241 4845
Fax +1 (312) 757 5553
usaoffice@kongnpark.com

South America: KONG & PARK CHILE SPA.
Presidente Riesco 5435, Of. 1601, Las Condes
Santiago, 7561127 Chile
Tel: +56 22 833 9055
chileoffice@kongnpark.com

Other countries: KONG & PARK, INC.
85, Gwangnaru-ro 56-gil, Prime center 1518
Gwangjin-gu, Seoul, 05116 Korea
Tel +82 (0)2 565 1531
Fax +82 (0)2 3445 1080
info@kongnpark.com

Printed in Korea

LEARNING KOREAN THROUGH TASKS:

HIGH BEGINNER TO LOW INTERMEDIATE

―실생활 태스크로 배우는 한국어―

LEARNING KOREAN THROUGH TASKS:
HIGH BEGINNER TO LOW INTERMEDIATE

Individual Speaking   Individual Writing   Collaborative Speaking   Collaborative Writing   Collaborative Speaking & Writing

TABLE OF CONTENTS

LEARNING KOREAN THROUGH TASKS:

HIGH BEGINNER TO LOW INTERMEDIATE

(::) Individual Speaking   📝 Individual Writing   💬 Collaborative Speaking   📝 Collaborative Writing   💬📝 Collaborative Speaking & Writing

Chapter	01	02	03	04
Genre	Posts on a Course Website	Emails	Text Messages	Social Media Posts
Pedagogic Tasks	💬📝 Write a Post about a Korean Lunar New Year (설날) Event You Attended	📝 Request an Override in a Korean Class	💬 Text a Friend about Spring Break	📝 Write a Social Media Post about a Family Trip
	📝 Write a Post about Memorable Events	📝 Apply for a Korean Study Abroad Program	📝 Text a Friend to Plan a Double Date	📝 Write a Social Media Post about Your High School Reunion
	(::) Create a Podcast about a Korean Cultural Event	💬 Present Study Abroad Program Experiences to Your Korean Professor	💬 Text a Friend to Plan a Study Session	(::) Post a Video on Social Media about Your High School Friends
Real World Task	(::) Make a Presentation to Introduce a Memorable Family Event	📝 Write an Email to Your Korean Professor	📝 Text a Friend to Make Plans for the Weekend	📝 Write a Social Media Post about a Memorable Event
Grammar Focus	1. Particle 한테 2. Particle 한테서 3. Clausal connective -지만 4. Honorific expressions: Word level 5. Subject honorific suffix -(으)시- 6. Noun-modifying form for adjective (present) -(으)ㄴ	1. Expressing desire -고 싶다 and -고 싶어 하다 2. Clausal connective -어/아서 3. Clausal connective -(으)ㄴ/는데 4. Noun-modifying form for verb (present) -는	1. Progressive form -고 있다 2. Particles (이)나, 밖에 3. Sentence ending -(으)ㄹ래요 4. Sentence ending -(으)ㄹ까요? 5. Particles A부터 B까지, A에서 B까지	1. Clausal connective -어/아서 2. Noun-modifying form for verb (past) -(으)ㄴ 3. ㅎ irregular 4. 'Wearing' verbs
Relevant Chapters in Other Textbooks	KL_B2 L9 AK_B2 L16 연세1 제3과 서강 1B CH2	KL_B2 L10 AK_B2 L11, L15 서강 1A CH6, 1B CH6, 2B CH1, 2B CH4	KL_B2 L11 AK_B1 L8, L10 연세1 제4과 서강 1B CH5, 2A CH2, 2A CH4	KL_B2 L12 AK_B2 L18 연세1 제6과 서강 2A CH3, 2B CH1

KL_B2 (KLEAR Integrated Korean Beginning 2), **AK_B1/B2** (Anytime Korean Beginning 1/2), **연세1** (연세 한국어1),
서강_1A/1B/2A/2B (서강 한국어1A/1B/2A/2B)

C O N T E N T O V E R V I E W

05	06	07	08
Phone Conversations	Postcards	Blogs	Vlogs
💬 Talk on the Phone to Plan Korean Cultural Festival Events	📝 Write a Postcard to Your Friend while Studying in Korea	📝 Write a Shopping Blog Post	💬 Make a Vlog Entry Comparing Korean Restaurants before Visiting
💬 Talk on the Phone to Discuss Changing a Presentation Date	📝 Write a Postcard to a Friend You Met during Study Abroad in Korea	📝 Write a Blog Post for a Moving Sale	💬 Make a Vlog Entry after Visiting a Korean Restaurant
💬 Leave a Voicemail Message to Request a Change in Presentation Date (Prerequisite: Chapter 05, Task 2)	💬 Send a Video Message to a Friend You Met during Study Abroad in Korea	💬 Create a Product Review Video on Your Shopping Blog	📝 Write a Vlog Entry Script about Visiting Korea
💬 Leave a Voicemail Message for Your Korean Professor	📝 Send a Postcard to Your Friend	💬 Create a Product Review Video on Your Shopping Blog	💬 Create a Vlog Entry about Your Favorite Places in Town
1. Benefactive expression -어/아 주다 2. Expressing obligation or necessity -어/아야 되다/하다 3. Causal expression Noun 때문에 4. Intentional -(으)ㄹ게요 5. Intentional -겠-	1. Causal expression Noun(이)라서 2. Negative expression -지 못하다 3. Negative command -지 말다 4. Adverbial suffix -게 5. 르 irregular 6. Clausal connective -(으)니까	1. Expressing ability/inability -(으)ㄹ 수 있다/없다 2. Clausal connective -(으)면서 3. Clausal connective -고 나서 4. Noun-modifying form for adjective/verb (future) -(으)ㄹ	1. Auxiliary verb -어/아 보다 2. Nominalization -기 3. Causal expression -기 때문에 4. Benefactive (humble) -어/아 드리다 5. Negative expression -지 않다
KL_B2 L13 AK_B2 L20 연세1 제8과 서강 1B CH4, CH7	KL_B2 L14 연세1 제7과 서강 1A CH6, 2A CH5	KL_B2 L15 연세1 제9과	KL_B2 L16 AK_B2 L15, L16, L20 서강 1B CH2, CH7

 Preface

Task-based language teaching (TBLT) has become one of the major approaches to teaching foreign and second languages in use today. Research within the fields of second language acquisition (SLA) and TBLT has provided evidence supporting the benefits of tasks in promoting language learning. Tasks are different from traditional language exercises in that they are meaning-oriented, have clear outcomes, and relate to real-world activities. Considering the benefits of tasks in foreign and second language instruction, "Learning Korean Through Tasks: High Beginner to Low Intermediate" is organized around a series of tasks. The target audience of the textbook includes high beginner to low intermediate Korean language learners in both Korean as a foreign language (KFL) and Korean as a second language (KSL) contexts.

The textbook presents pedagogic and real-world speaking and writing tasks as the basis of its organization. Because the textbook is for low-level learners, who are still in the process of learning new language features, we created tasks that elicit specific grammar and vocabulary features from students during task performance. Each task was thus designed as a "focused task," with particular target linguistic features in mind. All the tasks were carefully designed based on recent SLA and TBLT research findings. To offer additional information regarding the theoretical underpinnings of the design of the textbook, the next section presents a brief discussion of the tenets of TBLT.

Although recent classroom-based research has provided empirically-based recommendations for how to design and implement pedagogically sound tasks, such research findings have not been systemically incorporated into foreign language textbooks. This may be due to a lack of communication and/or collaboration between researchers and classroom practitioners. Our textbook development team, which consists of five authors, possesses the expertise to bridge this gap between foreign language research and pedagogy. YouJin Kim, a specialist in SLA and TBLT research, applies her knowledge of task-based approaches to Korean language pedagogy, resulting in a research-driven, task-supported course design. Bumyong Choi, the director of the Korean language program at Emory University, provides expertise in Korean linguistics and offers insights into practical concerns of implementing task-supported course curricula at the language-program level. Meanwhile, the wide range of teaching experience of Hyunae Yun, Binna Kim, and Sanghee Kang and their enthusiasm for task design have been invaluable assets to the project. The joint effort of these innovative scholars, whom we call the "Dream Team" of Korean TBLT curriculum design, demonstrates how three main stake holders—TBLT researchers, program directors, and classroom teachers—can work collaboratively towards the successful implementation of a TBLT curriculum project.

A defining characteristic of the textbook is that all tasks were designed, tested, and revised based on their use in actual Korean language classes. Since the initial design of the task-supported course syllabus in 2016, each task included in this book has been piloted and revised numerous times at Emory University in the USA. Through several rounds of pilot sessions, we collected students' task performance output and conducted reflection surveys. Based on students' perceptions of task effectiveness and their task performance, we evaluated the effectiveness and practicality of each task version and continuously revised them. Students new to TBLT may feel overwhelmed by the autonomy expected of them while completing tasks. However, as tasks are systematically incorporated into a task-supported syllabus throughout the semester, students will become more competent as task performers and will appreciate the sense of accomplishment they feel when they see the task outcomes. We believe that this iterative in-class task performance process will offer invaluable opportunities for using the Korean language in meaningful communicative contexts and will drive Korean-language learners to become Korean-language users.

To conclude, this project is one of the first attempts to introduce a task-based Korean textbook designed with the fundamental goal of connecting recent second language research and Korean language pedagogy. It is our hope that this is just the beginning of the production and use of task-based language textbooks. It has been a long journey involving many challenging "tasks" that required countless hours of "task engagement." However, we learned a great deal from every "task phase," and we are very humbled to share our "task outcome." We look forward to sharing a "post-task phase" with many of you in the future.

January 2021
YouJin Kim on behalf of the "Dream Team" of Korean TBLT Curriculum Design

Task-Based Approaches to Language Teaching

1. What are tasks?

Over the last few decades, task-based language teaching (TBLT) has received an increasing amount of attention in the field of second language (L2) acquisition and pedagogy (e.g., Ellis, 2003; Ellis, Skehan, Li, Shintani, & Lambert, 2020; Long, 2015, 2016; Samuda & Bygate, 2008; Van den Branden, 2006; Van den Branden, Bygate, & Norris, 2009). To date, researchers and L2 practitioners alike have offered a variety of definitions of "task." In the current book, we followed Van den Branden's (2006) definition of a task: "A task is an activity in which a person engages in order to attain an objective, and which necessitates the use of language" (p. 4). Furthermore, as guiding principles, the following characteristics were adopted when we were designing the tasks (Ellis, 2003, cited in Ellis & Shintani, 2014, p. 135):

(1) The primary focus should be on meaning.
(2) There should be some kind of gap (i.e., a need to convey information to express an opinion or to infer meaning).
(3) Learners should largely rely on their own linguistic and non-linguistic resources to complete the activity with some help from the task input.
(4) There is a clearly defined outcome other than the use of language.

In terms of implementing tasks, it is often advised to have three phases: pre-task, on-task, and post-task (see Table 1). We advise instructors to follow the proposed phases when implementing tasks in the classroom. At the pre-task phase, teachers provide general information about the task and activate students' schemata on task contexts. While students are performing tasks (on-task phase), teachers monitor students' task performance and provide corrective feedback if needed. During the post-task phase, students are invited to share their task outcomes, and teachers can prepare for form-focused language practice. For instance, teachers can review the errors that occurred most frequently during task performance based on their observation.

Table 1
Three-phase procedure (Adapted from Bygate, 2016)

Phase	Actions of Participants	
	Teacher	Students
Pre-task	• Providing general information about the task (purpose, conceptual content, expected outcome) • Presenting the input material	• Getting ready for task performance
On-task	• Monitoring students to offer support and clarification • Providing corrective feedback	• Engaging in the task
Post-task	• Providing form-focused language practice	• Reviewing task outcomes in terms of language use through teacher feedback or self-correction • Sharing task outcomes with the class

2. Task-based vs. task-supported curricula

Previous classroom-based studies have suggested possible modified forms of TBLT, taking different instructional contexts into consideration (i.e., localized TBLT, Kim, Jung, & Tracy-Ventura, 2017). These various forms of TBLT (e.g., task-based vs. task-supported language teaching) allow for instructors to enhance target grammar and vocabulary acquisition through the use of tasks. According to Samuda and Bygate (2008), task-based language teaching refers to "contexts where tasks are the central unit of instruction: they 'drive' classroom activity, they define curriculum and syllabuses, and they determine modes of assessment" (p. 58). Samuda and Bygate further describe task-based language teaching as follows (p. 58):

- Tasks define the language syllabus, with language being taught in response to the operational needs of specific learners.
- Tasks are seen as essential in engaging key processes of language acquisition.
- Tasks are selected on the basis that they replicate or simulate relevant real-world activities.
- Assessment is in terms of task performance.

On the other hand, task-supported language teaching refers to an approach that sees tasks as a main tool for language learning, used to enrich a syllabus or to provide additional learning opportunities. However, in such a scenario, tasks are not used as the main assessment tool. Samuda and Bygate (2008) describe task-supported language teaching in the following way (p. 60):

- Tasks are an important, but not the sole, element in a pedagogic cycle.
- Tasks are used in conjunction with different types of activities.
- Tasks are one element in the syllabus, but not necessarily the defining element.
- Tasks may be used as an element of assessment, but not necessarily as the defining element.

In task-supported language teaching, grammar and vocabulary can still guide syllabus design, while tasks can supplementally enhance the learning of target features.

Instructors and program directors can consider both approaches to teaching Korean using the current textbook. If the course curriculum is designed based on the tasks included in the book, a task-based approach to course development is appropriate. Otherwise, the tasks can be used to supplement another textbook to provide contexts for Korean language use and acquisition.

3. Unfocused tasks vs. focused tasks

According to Ellis (2009), tasks can be categorized as unfocused or focused. Unfocused tasks promote learners' use of language communicatively without predetermined linguistic targets. Thus, learners would produce relevant language features naturally as they are needed in the process of completing tasks. On the other hand, focused tasks provide learners with opportunities to use particular task-induced linguistic features. The pedagogic tasks included in the current textbook were designed as focused tasks to address instructors' concern, "What if students do not use target grammar and vocabulary while completing tasks?" This is probably one of the most common concerns among instructors, particularly in low-level foreign language classroom contexts where tasks are implemented. During the pilot stage of this textbook, we addressed this concern by incorporating more controlled task input.

4. Theoretical rationale for task approaches to teaching and learning Korean

Thanks to the pedagogical benefits of tasks, with the aforementioned characteristics and components in mind, tasks have come to be considered one of the major means by which instructors conduct language teaching. Besides being effective for achieving particular pedagogical purposes, the use of tasks in classroom contexts is well supported by various SLA theories and empirical classroom-based research on how language learning happens (Ellis, 2017; Ellis & Shintani, 2014; Ellis, Skehan, Li, Shintani, & Lambert, 2020; Van den Branden, Bygate, & Norris, 2009).

Among many SLA theories, research from the cognitive-interactionist perspective and sociocultural theory has provided increasing support for task-based language teaching (Ellis & Shintani, 2014). More specifically, from cognitive-interactionist perspectives, tasks provide input, interaction, and output opportunities, which are necessary processes for language learning. During tasks, learners are able to notice necessary linguistic forms while focusing on meaning. Additionally, since tasks are designed based on learners' real-world needs and interests, it is expected that such task characteristics will motivate learners to be engaged with the language, which is necessary to achieve task goals. From sociocultural theory perspectives, tasks offer contexts where learners mediate with objects, others, and themselves, which are key learning mechanisms. Furthermore, during collaborative tasks, learners can provide each other with assistance, known as scaffolding, while solving linguistic problems.

Following the above-mentioned theoretical frameworks, numerous empirical studies have been conducted (See Ellis, 2017; Kim, 2015; Long, 2015, 2016), and have not only supported the use of tasks in language learning, but have also offered various suggestions about how to design and sequence tasks for optimal language learning. In the context of Korean instruction, previous research has focused on (1) comparing individual and collaborative tasks (Cho & Kim, in press; Kim, 2008), (2) examining the role of interlocutor variables (e.g., proficiency level and heritage vs. non-heritage status; Kim & McDonough, 2008; Kim, Lee, & Kim, 2018), (3) investigating the effects of task repetition (Kim, Choi, Yun, Kim, & Choi, in press; Kim, Kang, Yun, Kim, & Choi, in press), and (4) exploring the role of synchronous corrective feedback as a way to promote engagement with language during task performance (Kim, Choi, Kang, Kim, & Yun, 2020). Some of these studies were conducted as a part of a large pilot study for the current textbook project. Some of the major findings of previous task-based research focusing on Korean instruction are as follows:

(1) Both individual and collaborative tasks encouraged students to pay attention to task-induced language features (Kim, 2008).
(2) Collaborative tasks promoted a greater degree of vocabulary learning than individual tasks (Kim, 2008).
(3) Collaborative tasks and individual tasks similarly promoted the learning of honorifics through email-writing tasks (Cho & Kim, in press).
(4) Exact task repetition (repeating the exact same task twice) improved writing fluency (Kim, Choi, Yun, Kim, & Choi, in press).
(5) Exact task repetition benefitted syntactic complexity, but little evidence of benefits of global accuracy was found (Kim, Kang, Yun, Kim, & Choi, in press).
(6) Procedural repetition (repeating the procedure of a task with different content) resulted in a greater degree of grammar learning compared to exact task repetition (Kim, Kang, Yun, Kim, & Choi, in press).
(7) Synchronous written corrective feedback (e.g., circling errors on students' writing while they are performing writing tasks) facilitated accuracy in students' writing as well as learning of grammar (Kim, Choi, Kang, Kim, & Yun, 2020; Kim, Choi, Yun, Kim, & Choi, in press).

Based on the current trends of using tasks in language teaching, many English as a Second Language (ESL) textbooks have adopted pedagogic tasks which promote learners' use of language in meaningful contexts and thus stimulate learner's language learning autonomy. Although such noticeable changes have taken place in English as a foreign or second language pedagogy, Korean language materials have not yet been created. There have been a few attempts to implement tasks in Korean language curricula, but most of them have been limited to advanced Korean language programs (e.g., Kong, 2012) or ended after the conclusion of a research project (e.g., Chaudron et al., 2005). To date, there have not been any reported cases of TBLT being used in an elementary-level Korean curriculum. Learners' limited proficiency in the target language makes it difficult to develop authentic or meaningful tasks at this level. However, the current trend in language pedagogy emphasizes the importance of language use in real-life tasks by promoting the 5 Cs (Communication, Culture, Comparison, Connection, and Community) in all levels of language curricula (The National Standards Collaborative Board, 2015). The Standards-Based College Curriculum for Korean Language Education (AATK, 2015) provides clear guidelines for using meaningful tasks even in elementary-level curricula. Furthermore, previous research has demonstrated that low-level (i.e., high beginner and low intermediate) Korean language learners can benefit from performing tasks in terms of learning new grammar, vocabulary, and pragmatics. We took these findings into consideration when we designed the current textbook in order to make a clear connection between TBLT research and Korean language pedagogy. We hope that this book inspires further development of TBLT materials that are empirically-tested and motivated.

✓ Highlights of the Book

In the current, rapidly-changing digital era, multimodality (i.e., the use of different semiotic modes, such as pictures, texts, and music when making meaning) and diverse genres of speaking and writing tasks are required in real-world language use contexts. *Learning Korean Through Tasks* consists of eight chapters which present a total of 32 tasks that were designed based on on-going needs analysis. Although the list is not exhaustive, our book is organized around the major communication genres and modes that are common in the lives of the target students: posts on a course website, emails, text messages, social media posts, phone conversations, postcards, blogs, and vlogs.

One key feature of this textbook is that all the materials were designed based on current SLA theories and research findings, incorporating the importance of input, output, noticing, and interaction, the important functions of each task phase, the importance of considering task complexity levels, the importance of task repetition, and the importance of an integrated approach to language teaching by incorporating elements of speaking, writing, reading, and listening during task performance. Furthermore, the importance of task transferability between pedagogic tasks and real-world tasks is a key feature of the textbook. The tasks in the book are sequenced according to their genre and target-task outcomes. Although the task materials were originally created to coincide with the chapters in one of the KLEAR textbooks published by the University of Hawai'i Press (*Integrated Korean Beginning 2*), each task has its own module with the required target grammar and key expressions, which makes our textbook flexible and an option for use by learners that do not use *Integrated Korean Beginning 2* as their textbook.

Highlights of the organization of each chapter

(1) All tasks were designed as focused tasks, which require task-induced grammar and vocabulary features in order to complete the tasks. In other words, the tasks naturally elicit these grammar and vocabulary features as the students complete them. Each chapter starts with the section "Grammar Focus," which introduces the target grammar features of the chapter.

(2) Each task starts with a "Task Scenario," followed by "Grammar in Action" and "Helpful Words and Expressions," which provide language resources for task completion.

(3) Each chapter consists of four tasks: three pedagogic tasks and one real-world task. The main learning outcome of each chapter is students' successful completion of the real-world task. Building on the pedagogic tasks, the real-world task can be performed using student-generated content and task input. This design sequence promotes clear task transferability between pedagogic task performance and real-world task performance in each chapter.

(4) For every chapter, we provide both speaking and writing tasks in various formats, such as individual speaking, individual writing, collaborative speaking, collaborative writing, and collaborative speaking & writing. Each task type requires different steps:

- Individual speaking tasks: planning, rehearsing, recording;
- Individual writing tasks: planning and writing;
- Collaborative speaking tasks: planning, sharing/rehearsing, recording;
- Collaborative writing tasks: planning and writing;
- Collaborative speaking & writing tasks: planning, sharing, writing.

☑ How to Use this Book

The target audience of our textbook are high-beginner and low-intermediate-level learners. The textbook can be used as a main textbook in both Korean as a foreign language and Korean as a second language contexts where a task-based syllabus is adopted. Additionally, because the target grammar features of each task unit mostly mirror those used in KLEAR's *Integrated Korean: Beginning 2* (3rd Edition), our book may be used as a supplement to that text, as well as to any other Korean language-learning textbook of a similar level.

The textbook is organized around different task genres. Each chapter includes four tasks: three pedagogic tasks and one real-world task. Building on students' task performance experience with Tasks 1-3, the real-world task requires students to create their own task content using their own materials.

이 교재는 다양한 태스크 유형들로 구성되어 있습니다. 교재에는 다양한 태스크 장르들이 있고, 각 챕터는 3개의 '교수용 목적의 태스크 (pedagogic task)'와 1개의 '실제 활용 태스크(real-world task)' 이렇게 총 4개의 태스크로 구성되어 있습니다. 교수용 목적의 태스크 (Task 1~Task 3)는 학습자들의 태스크 수행 능력을 높이기 위한 태스크이고 실제 활용 태스크(Task 4)는 학습자들이 자신의 이야기만으로 온전히 완성해 보는 태스크입니다.

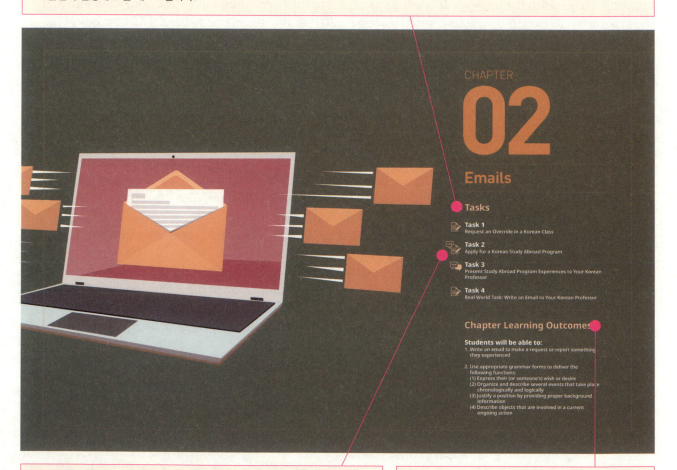

CHAPTER

02

Emails

Tasks

📱 **Task 1**
Request an Override in a Korean Class

💬 **Task 2**
Apply for a Korean Study Abroad Program

📱 **Task 3**
Present Study Abroad Program Experiences to Your Korean Professor

📝 **Task 4**
Real World Task: Write an Email to Your Korean Professor

Chapter Learning Outcomes

Students will be able to:
1. Write an email to make a request or report something they experienced

2. Use appropriate grammar forms to deliver the following functions:
   (1) Express their (or someone's) wish or desire
   (2) Organize and describe several events that take place chronologically and logically
   (3) Justify a position by providing proper background information
   (4) Describe objects that are involved in a current ongoing action

There are five task types: individual speaking (📱), individual writing (📝), collaborative speaking (💬), collaborative writing (📝), and collaborative speaking & writing (📝). Each task type is indicated using emoticons.

이 교재의 태스크 타입은 개인말하기(📱), 개인작문(📝), 협동말하기(💬), 협동작문(📝), 협동말하기와 작문(📝) 이렇게 모두 5가지입니다. 각 태스크 타입은 이모티콘으로 표현됩니다.

Chapter learning outcomes are determined based on what students will be able to produce (e.g., an email) and on the linguistic and non-linguistic learning goals of the task.

각 과의 학습 결과는 이메일 쓰기와 같이 실제 산출되는 결과물과 언어적, 비언어적 학습목표들의 성과를 기반으로 하여 결정됩니다.

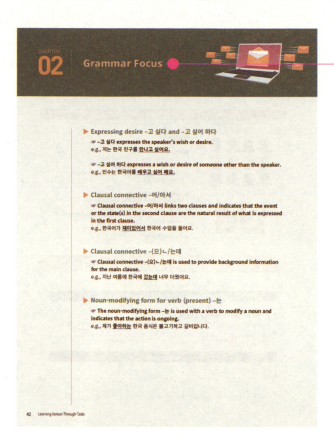

Each chapter starts with "Grammar Focus." It introduces the grammar features that are required for task completion in that chapter's tasks.

각 챕터의 첫 장에는 Grammar Focus 부분이 제시되어 있습니다. 각 챕터의 태스크 수행 시 필수적으로 써야 하는 문법들을 간략한 설명 및 예문으로 제시해 놓았습니다.

Task type (individual speaking, individual writing, collaborative speaking, collaborative writing, collaborative speaking & writing) is indicated after each task title.

각 태스크 제목 아래에 태스크 타입(개인말하기, 개인작문, 협동말하기, 협동작문, 협동말하기와 작문)이 제시되어 있습니다.

Each task is introduced using task scenarios which present the context of the task. For task authenticity, all scenarios were written based on students' daily use of Korean and English as reported in their needs analysis.

모든 태스크에는 태스크 시나리오가 있습니다. 교재의 모든 태스크 시나리오들은 학생들이 한국이나 영어권 생활환경에서 마주칠 수 있는 자연스러운 상황들로 구성하여 태스크의 실제성을 높였습니다.

Grammar features and vocabulary words that are helpful for task performance are introduced in "Grammar in Action" and "Helpful Words & Expressions."

학생들의 태스크 수행에 도움을 줄 수 있는 문법과 단어들이 각각 "Grammar in Action"과 "Helpful Words & Expressions"에 소개되어 있습니다.

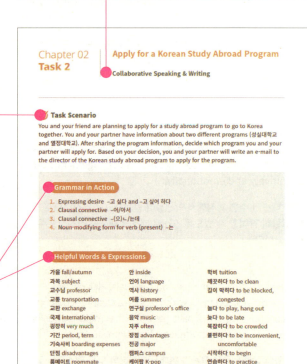

Chapter 02
Task 2

Apply for a Korean Study Abroad Program

Collaborative Speaking & Writing

Task Scenario

You and your friend are planning to apply for a study abroad program to go to Korea together. You and your partner have information about two different programs (성실대학교 and 열정대학교). After sharing the program information, decide which program you and your partner will apply for. Based on your decision, you and your partner will write an e-mail to the director of the Korean study abroad program to apply for the program.

Grammar in Action

1. Expressing desire –고 싶다 and –고 싶어 하다
2. Clausal connective –어/아서
3. Clausal connective –(으)ㄴ/는데
4. Noun-modifying form for verb (present) –는

Helpful Words & Expressions

가을 fall/autumn	안 inside	학비 tuition
과목 subject	언어 language	깨끗하다 to be clean
교수님 professor	역사 history	길이 막히다 to be blocked,
교통 transportation	여름 summer	congested
교환 exchange	연구실 professor's office	놀다 to play, hang out
국제 international	음악 music	늦다 to be late
굉장히 very much	자주 often	복잡하다 to be crowded
기간 period, term	장점 advantages	불편하다 to be inconvenient,
기숙사비 boarding expenses	전공 major	uncomfortable
단점 disadvantages	캠퍼스 campus	시작하다 to begin
룸메이트 roommate	케이팝 K-pop	연습하다 to practice
문화 culture	클럽 club	(에) 지원하다 to apply
메뉴 menu	프로그램 program	죄송하다 to be sorry
밖 outside	택시 taxi	편하다 to be convenient,
스터디 어브로드 study abroad	학기 semester	comfortable

46   Learning Korean Through Tasks

This textbook includes many collaborative tasks. If a task is a collaborative task, Student A and Student B receive different types of information, which will require students to exchange information in Korean. In this case, Student A has information about 성실대학교, whereas Student B has information about 열정대학교.

이 교재에는 협동 태스크가 다수 있습니다. 협동 태스크의 경우, 학생A와 학생B는 서로 다른 정보를 받고 한국어로 서로 정보를 교환하여(정보차 활동) 태스크를 수행하도록 구성되어 있습니다. 예를 들어, 학생A는 성실대학교에 대한 정보를, 학생B는 열정대학교에 대한 정보를 받은 상태인데, 학생A와 학생B는 서로의 정보를 한국어로 교환하여 태스크를 완성시켜야 합니다.

All tasks start with a "planning stage," which usually takes about 5 minutes. During this stage, students create task content using the task input.

태스크를 수행하기 위해 태스크를 준비하는 단계로서, 학생들에게 약 5분의 시간이 주어집니다. 이 단계에서 학생들은 주어진 태스크 인풋(task input)을 활용하여 태스크 수행에 필요한 내용들을 미리 구상하게 됩니다.

When more than two clauses are required, for example when using connectives such as -(으)ㄴ/는데 and 어/아서, we remind students of that by indicating clause 1 and clause 2 in the task input.

학생들에게 -(으)ㄴ/는데, 어/아서 등의 연결어미로 두 개 이상의 구를 쓰도록 하기 위해 clause 1, clause 2 등을 표기함으로써 목표 문법을 도출하도록 했습니다.

For all tasks, students are required to come up with task content on their own to increase task engagement both cognitively and emotionally.

모든 태스크 수행 과정에서 학생들이 인지적으로 감성적으로 더욱 활발히 참여할 수 있도록 스스로 태스크 내용을 작성하도록 하였습니다.

To encourage student interaction, virtually all tasks are designed as closed tasks which require a clear task outcome. For collaborative tasks, pairs have to either make a decision together or present information from both students.

학생들의 상호작용을 북돋기 위해서 대부분의 모든 태스크는 결론을 도출해야 하는 "closed task"로 디자인되었습니다. 예를 들어 협동 태스크의 경우, 학생들은 서로의 태스크 인풋에서 알맞은 정보를 교환해야 하거나 토론 후 결론을 도출해 내야 합니다.

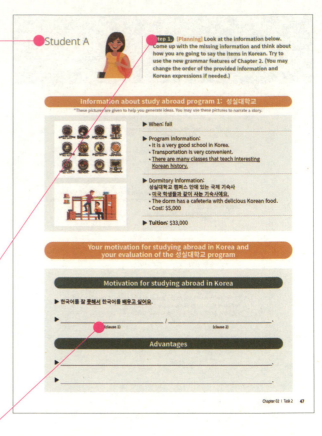

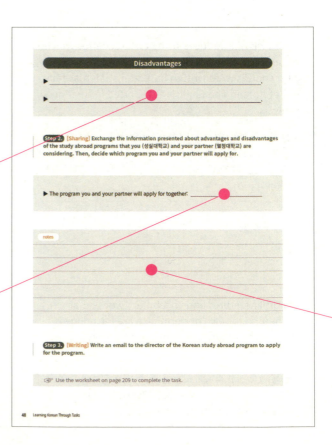

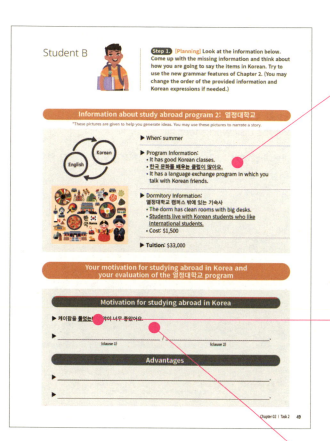

We intentionally mixed Korean and English input. Students are exposed to the target grammar feature at least once in Korean (e.g., 한국 문화를 **배우는** 클럽이 많아요). Additionally, in order to ensure that students are able to use the target grammar and vocabulary during task performance, we used English input to control the content of the tasks to some extent.

태스크 인풋은 한국어 혹은 영어로 혼합되어 제공됩니다. 그리고 학습자들에게 그 챕터의 목표 문법(target grammar feature)이 적어도 한 번은 한국어 인풋으로 노출되도록 인풋의 수를 조정하였습니다(예: 한국 문화를 **배우는** 클럽이 많아요.). 또한 학생들이 각 챕터의 목표 문법 및 단어들을 사용하게끔 일부 태스크의 내용을 영어 인풋으로 제공하는 형식으로 태스크 내용을 일부 제한하였습니다.

Among Korean input, target grammar features are underlined and presented in bold in order to raise students' awareness of target grammar features.

한국어 인풋 중에서 목표 문법에 해당하는 부분에는 굵은 글씨와 밑줄 처리를 하여 학생들에게 그 챕터에서 습득해야 할 목표 문법이 인지적으로 노출되게 하였습니다.

For collaborative tasks, we diversified task input between the two students (Student A and Student B) so that the target grammar and vocabulary are distributed equally.

특히 협동 태스크의 경우, 목표 문법이나 단어의 한국어 노출이 두 학생(학생A와 학생B)에게 고르게 분포되도록 구성하였습니다.

Students can use this space to take notes while preparing task content before they perform writing or speaking tasks on a separate task worksheet.

학생들은 작문 태스크를 시작하기 전 혹은 말하기 태스크를 녹음하기 전에 notes 공간을 사용하여 미리 태스크를 준비할 수 있습니다.

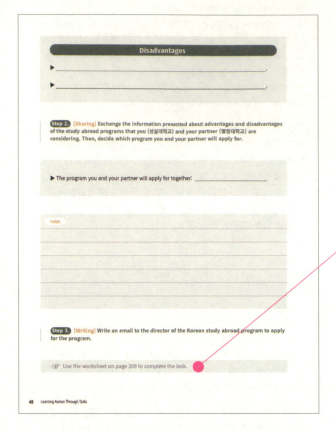

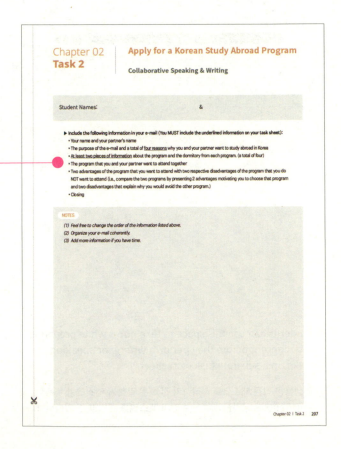

When students are ready to begin recording or writing the task content, they are asked to complete the task using the task worksheet.

학생들이 말하기 녹음이나 쓰기를 할 준비가 되면 태스크 활동지로 이동합니다.

On the task worksheet, students are reminded of the required information for task completion. Students can reorder the information if necessary.

태스크 활동지에는 태스크 완성을 위해 꼭 들어가야 할 내용이 다시 한 번 요약되어 있습니다. 일부 태스크의 경우, 학생들이 정보의 순서를 자유롭게 바꿀 수 있습니다.

✓ Useful Information regarding How to Interpret Task Input

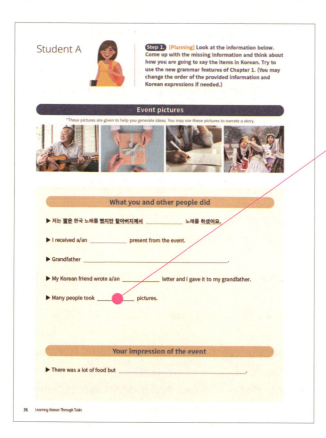

The blank spaces in the task input encourage the students to develop content according to their own understanding of each situation. For instance, this space indicates that students must come up with a noun modifier (e.g., adjective such as 예쁜).

밑줄 형태의 빈칸들은 학생들이 태스크 시나리오를 고려하여 스스로 적절한 내용을 구성하는 공간입니다. 예컨대, 이 예시의 빈칸(밑줄)에는 명사를 수식하는 형용사 관형형을 써야 하는데, 여러 형용사 관형형 중 학생들이 상황에 가장 적절한 형용사 관형형을 스스로 생각해 내어 쓰도록 유도하고 있습니다.

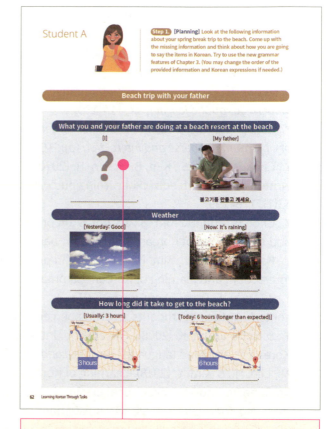

There is a question mark (?) and a blank space in the task input when students have to come up with the content on their own.

학생들이 태스크 내용 자체를 생각해 내야 하는 경우에는 다음과 같은 물음표(?) 형태로 제시했습니다.

Task worksheets present the real-world task output format.

태스크 활동지는 실생활에서 쓰이는 양식을 바탕으로 구성되었습니다.

✅ References

Bygate, M. (2016). Sources, developments and directions of task-based language teaching. *The Language Learning Journal, 44*(4), 381–400.

Chaudron, C., Doughty, C., Kim, Y., Kong, D., Lee, J., Lee, Y., & Urano, K. (2005). A task-based needs analysis of a tertiary Korean as a foreign language program. In M. Long (Ed.), *Second language needs analysis* (pp. 225-262). Cambridge University Press.

Cho, H., & Kim, Y. (in press). Learning Korean honorifics through individual and collaborative writing tasks and written corrective feedback. *Applied Linguistics Review*.

Ellis, R. (2003). *Task-based language learning and teaching*. Oxford University Press.

Ellis, R. (2009). Task-based language teaching: Sorting out the misunderstandings. *International Journal of Applied Linguistics*, *19*, 221-246.

Ellis, R. (2017). Moving task-based language teaching forward. *Language Teaching*, *50*, 507-526.

Ellis, R., & Shintani, N. (2014). *Exploring language pedagogy through second language acquisition research*. Routledge.

Ellis, R., Skehan, P., Li, S., Shintani, N., & Lambert, C. (2020). *Task-based language teaching: Theory and practice*. Cambridge University Press.

Kim, Y. (2008). The contribution of collaborative and individual tasks to the acquisition of L2 vocabulary. *Modern Language Journal*, *92*, 114-130.

Kim, Y. (2015). The role of tasks as vehicles for learning in classroom interaction. In N. Markee (Ed.), *Handbook of classroom discourse and interaction* (pp. 163-181). Wiley-Blackwell.

Kim, Y., Choi, B., Kang, S., Kim, B., & Yun, H. (2020). Comparing the effects of direct and indirect synchronous written corrective feedback: Learning outcomes and students' perceptions. *Foreign Language Annals*, *53*(1), 176–199.

Kim, Y., Choi, B., Yun, H., Kim, B., & Choi, S. (in press). Task repetition, synchronous written corrective feedback and the learning of Korean: A classroom-based study. *Language Teaching Research*.

Kim, Y., Kang, S., Yun, H., Kim, B., & Choi, B. (in press). The effects of task repetition on writing quality, peer interaction, and learning of Korean grammar. *Foreign Language Annals*.

Kim, Y., Jung, Y., & Tracy - Ventura, N. (2017). Implementation of a localized task - based course in an EFL context: A study of students' evolving perceptions. *TESOL Quarterly*, *51*(3), 632-660.

Kim, Y., & McDonough, K. (2008). The effect of interlocutor proficiency on the collaborativedialogue between Korean as a second language learners. *Language Teaching Research*, *12*, 211-234.

Kim, M., Lee, H., & Kim, Y. (2018). Learning of Korean honorifics through collaborative tasks: Comparing heritage and non-Heritage speakers. In. N. Taguchi & Y. Kim (Eds.). *Task-based approaches to teaching and assessing pragmatics* (pp. 28-54). Amsterdam: John Benjamins.

Kong, D. (2012). Task-based language teaching in an advanced Korean language learning program. *The Korean Language in America*, *17*, 32-48.

Long, M. (2015). *Second language acquisition and task-based language teaching*. Wiley-Blackwell.

Long, M. (2016). In defense of tasks and TBLT: Nonissues and real issues. *Annual Review of Applied Linguistics*, *36*, 5-33.

Samuda, V., & Bygate, M. (2008). *Tasks in second language learning*. Palgrave.

The National Standards Collaborative Board. (2015). *World-readiness standards for learning languages* (4th ed).

Van den Branden, K. (Ed.). (2006). *Task-based language teaching in practice*. Cambridge University Press.

Van den Branden, K., Bygate, M., & Norris, J. M. (Eds.). (2009). *Task-based language teaching: A reader*. John Benjamins.

⊘ Acknowledgements

It has been a long journey to arrive at the completion of *Learning Korean Through Tasks: High Beginner to Low Intermediate*. Without many individuals' support, this fruitful outcome would not have been possible. First, we would like to thank the Emory University students who were enrolled in KRN 102 and participated in the pilot studies. The tasks have been through numerous rounds of revisions based on students' task performance and valuable comments, which helped us immensely to improve the quality of each task. Secondly, special thanks go to Sujeong Choi and Meredith D'Arienzo who helped to revise the tasks and provided valuable comments throughout the task piloting process and textbook writing. Special thanks also go to Mr. Kyung Yong Kong and Ms. Yejoo Lee from the Kong & Park publishing company who have always been enthusiastic about the textbook project and who offered endless support, without which this final outcome would not have been possible. Finally, we would like to thank the Center for Urban Language Teaching and Research at Georgia State University for providing research funding for the project and the Department of Russian and East Asian Languages and Cultures at Emory University for providing professional development funding for publishing this book.

CHAPTER

01

Posts on a Course Website

Tasks

 Task 1
Write a Post about a Korean Lunar New Year (설날)
Event You Attended

 Task 2
Write a Post about Memorable Events

 Task 3
Create a Podcast about a Korean Cultural Event

 Task 4
Real World Task: Make a Presentation to Introduce
a Memorable Family Event

Chapter Learning Outcomes

Students will be able to:

1. Narrate an event that they experienced in both
   oral and written communication forms

2. Use appropriate grammar forms to deliver the
   following functions:
   (1) Describe actions in which someone passes
   something to a recipient
   (2) Describe someone's actions in a polite way
   (3) Describe objects with detail
   (4) Contrast two situations or actions

Grammar Focus

▶ Particle 한테

☞ **Particle 한테 indicates that the noun with it is affected by actions in the sentence.**
e.g., 미나가 **민수한테** 크리스마스 카드를 줬어요.

▶ Particle 한테서

☞ **Particle 한테서 indicates that the noun with it is the source of actions or situations in the sentence.**
e.g., 미나가 **민수한테서** 선물을 받았어요.

▶ Clausal connective –지만

☞ **Clausal connective –지만 is used to indicate a contrast between two clauses.**
e.g., 신발이 **예쁘지만** 조금 비싸요.

▶ Honorific expressions: Word level

☞ **Some Korean words have equivalent honorific counterparts.**

한테 or 한테서	께 (to/from)	나이	연세 (age)
이/가	께서 (subject honorific)	이름	성함 (name)
은/는	께서는 (subject honorific + topic)	집	댁 (home)

▶ Subject honorific suffix –(으)시–

☞ **Subject honorific suffix –(으)시– is used when the speaker wants to express politeness to the subject of the sentence or the referent of the topic.**
e.g., 아버지께서 신문을 **읽으십니다.**

▶ Noun-modifying form for adjective (present) –(으)ㄴ

☞ **If –(으)ㄴ is used with an adjective, it modifies a noun (i.e., noun-modifying form) and indicates its current state.**
e.g., 어머니께서 저한테 **따뜻한** 장갑을 주셨어요.

Write a Post about a Korean Lunar New Year (설날) Event You Attended
Collaborative Speaking & Writing

 Task Scenario

You and your partner went to a Korean Lunar New Year (설날) event for your Korean class team project. The event was held for two days. You went on the first day of the event, and your partner went on the second day. For a team project, you and your partner will introduce your Korean friend's grandmother, who hosted the event and describe what you and other people did at the event. Then you and your partner will write a post about the event for your course website.

Grammar in Action

1. Particle 한테
2. Particle 한테서
3. Clausal connective –지만
4. Honorific expressions: Word level
5. Subject honorific suffix –(으)시–
6. Noun-modifying form for adjective (present) –(으)ㄴ

Helpful Words & Expressions

댁 house (honorific)
떡국 rice cake soup
사람들 people
선물 present, gift
성함 name (honorific)
스웨터 sweater
연세 age (honorific)
음식 food
이벤트 event
장갑 gloves
길다 to be long

드리다 to give (humble)
드시다 to eat (honorific)
따뜻하다 to be warm
많다 to be many, much
비싸다 to be expensive
사진을 찍다 to take a picture
시끄럽다 to be noisy
신나다 to be excited
싸다 to be cheap
음식을 만들다 to make food
이야기를 듣다 to hear a story

재미없다 to be boring
재미있다 to be fun
적다 to be little, few
주시다 to give (honorific)
즐겁다 to be joyful
짧다 to be short
카드를 쓰다 to write a card

Student A

Step 1. [Planning] Look at the information below. Come up with the missing information and think about how you are going to say the items in Korean. Try to use the new grammar features of Chapter 1. (You may change the order of the provided information and Korean expressions if needed.)

Event pictures

*These pictures are given to help you generate ideas. You may use these pictures to narrate a story.

What you and other people did

▶ 저는 **짧은** 한국 노래를 **했지만 할아버지께서** _____ 노래를 **하셨어요.**

▶ I received a/an _____ present from the event.

▶ Grandfather _____.

▶ My Korean friend wrote a/an _____ letter and I gave it to my grandfather.

▶ Many people took _____ pictures.

Your impression of the event

▶ There was a lot of food but _____.

Step 2. [Sharing] Using the information presented, share your experience of the event with your partner. Also, you and your partner met your Korean friend's grandmother, who hosted the event. However, you and your partner have different information about her. Talk about her while exchanging the following information.

Information about Korean friend's grandmother

Name: 김은주   Age: Birthday: June 18th

notes

Step 3. [Writing] In pairs, write a post about the Lunar New Year (설날) event that you attended.

☞ Use the worksheet on page 193 to complete the task.

Student B

Step 1. [Planning] Look at the information below. Come up with the missing information and think about how you are going to say the items in Korean. Try to use the new grammar features of Chapter 1. (You may change the order of the provided information and Korean expressions if needed.)

Event pictures

*These pictures are given to help you generate ideas. You may use these pictures to narrate a story.

What you and other people did

▶ **할머니께서는 저한테** _____ 을/를 **주시고** 저는 할머니**께** _____ 장갑을 **드렸어요**.

▶ I listended to _____ 설날(Lunar New Year) stories told by a Korean teacher.

▶ Grandmother made _____ 떡국(rice cake soup) and she _____.

▶ Many people listened to _____ Korean music.

Your impression of the event

▶ The event was joyful but _____.

Step 2. [Sharing] Using the information presented, share your experience of the event with your partner. Also, you and your partner met your Korean friend's grandmother who hosted the event. However, you and your partner have different information about her. Talk about her while exchanging the following information.

Information about Korean friend's grandmother

Name: Age: 79   Birthday:

notes

_____

_____

_____

_____

_____

_____

_____

_____

_____

_____

_____

Step 3. [Writing] In pairs, write a post about the Lunar New Year (설날) event that you attended.

☞ Use the worksheet on page 193 to complete the task.

Chapter 01
Task 2

Write a Post about Memorable Events
Individual Writing

✅ Task Scenario

You are going to write a post about the two most memorable events that you have ever attended. You will introduce when and where the events were held. Also, you will describe what you and other people did at the events and how you felt about the events.

Grammar in Action

1. Particle 한테
2. Particle 한테서
3. Clausal connective –지만
4. Honorific expressions: Word level
5. Subject honorific suffix –(으)시–
6. Noun-modifying form for adjective (present) –(으)ㄴ

Helpful Words & Expressions

날씨 weather

댁 house (honorific)

두 번째 second

생신 birthday (honorific)

월 month (counter)

일 day (counter)

진지 meal (honorific)

첫 번째 first

카드 card

크리스마스 Christmas

파티 party

길다 to be long

드리다 to give (humble)

드시다 to eat (honorific)

멋지다 to be nice

비싸다 to be expensive

사진을 찍다 to take a picture

소개하다 to introduce

예쁘다 to be pretty

음식을 만들다 to make food

이야기를 하다 to talk, tell
      a story

재미없다 to be boring

재미있다 to be fun

주무시다 to sleep (honorific)

주시다 to give (honorific)

즐겁다 to be joyful

짧다 to be short

춥다 to be cold

Christmas party

*These pictures are given to help you generate ideas. You may use these pictures to narrate a story

| When | _____ 월 _____ 일 |
| Where | My parents' house |

What you did

▶ I gave a/an _____ Christmas card to my parents.

What other people did

▶ **할머니께서** _____ 음식을 **드셨어요**.

▶ My mother took a/an _____ picture and **저한테 주셨어요**.

▶ My father _____.

Your impression of the event

▶ 날씨가 **추웠지만** _____.

▶ The event was long but _____.

Grandfather's birthday

*These pictures are given to help you generate ideas. You may use these pictures to narrate a story

When _____ 월 _____ 일

Where _____

What you did

▶ 저는 **할아버지께 큰** 선물을 **드렸어요**.

What other people did

▶ My grandfather told _____ stories to us.

▶ My grandmother read a/an _____ book and gave it to me.

▶ My mother _____.

Your impression of the event

▶ The birthday party was joyful but _____.

Step 2. [Writing] Write a post to describe your memorable events.

☞ Use the worksheet on page 197 to complete the task.

Create a Podcast about a Korean Cultural Event
Individual Speaking

 Task Scenario

You attended a Korean cultural event at your university. There were many booths that introduced Korean culture, and you participated in two booths. You will create a short podcast about the Korean cultural event as a project for your Korean course. In your podcast, you will describe the two booths that you participated in and where the event was held. Also, you will describe what you and other people did at the event and how you felt about it.

Grammar in Action

1. Particle 한테
2. Particle 한테서
3. Clausal connective –지만
4. Honorific expressions: Word level
5. Subject honorific suffix –(으)시–
6. Noun-modifying form for adjective (present) –(으)ㄴ

Helpful Words & Expressions

교수님 professor
그림 picture/drawing
날씨 weather
떡 rice cake
부스 booth
이벤트 event
책갈피 bookmark
카드 card
탁자 table
한국 문화 Korean culture
학생회관 student center
길다 to be long

덥다 to be hot
드리다 to give (humble)
드시다 to eat (honorific)
많다 to be many
맛없다 to taste bad
맛있다 to be delicious
멋지다 to be nice
사진을 찍다 to take a picture
신나다 to be excited
아름답다 to be beautiful
음식을 만들다 to make food

(하고) 이야기하다 to talk (with)
작다 to be small
재미없다 to be boring
재미있다 to be fun
적다 to be little, few
주시다 to give (honorific)
즐겁다 to be joyful
짧다 to be short
춥다 to be cold
크다 to be big
행복하다 to be happy

When _____ 월 _____ 일

Where 학생회관

Event booth 1

Things at the event site

▶ **많은** 사람들

▶ _____ pictures

▶ _____ tables

What you and other people did

*These pictures are given to help you generate ideas. You may use these pictures to narrate a story.

▶ I wrote _____ card and **김 선생님께** 그 카드를 **드렸어요**.

▶ My Korean teacher made a Korean bookmark and s/he _____.

▶ **박 교수님께서 저희한테** 한국 문화를 **이야기하셨어요**.

Event booth 2

Things at the event site

▶ delicious food

▶ _____ games

▶ _____ music

What you and other people did

▶ I made _____ 떡(rice cake) and gave it to my friend.

▶ The Korean 101 teacher ate the rice cake and s/he _____.

▶ Professor Choi _____.

Your impression of the event

▶ 이벤트에 음식이 **많았지만** _____.

▶ The weather _____ but the event was so interesting.

Step 2. [Rehearsing] **Rehearse a podcast about the Korean cultural event using the information presented. You can take notes to organize your podcast.**

Helpful questions to elicit the content of your podcast

▶ What is your name? (Personal introduction of yourself)

▶ What was the event that you attended?

▶ When and where was the event held?

▶ What was at the event site? (e.g., 많은 음식이 있었어요.)

▶ What did you and other people (e.g., 선생님, 교수님) do at each booth?

▶ What was your opinion/impression of the event?

notes

Step 3. [Recording] **Record your podcast using your notes above.**

☞ Use the worksheet on page 201 to complete the task.

Make a Presentation to Introduce a Memorable Family Event
Individual Speaking

 Task Scenario

You are going to make a presentation to introduce a memorable family event. Choose one past family event in which you participated. Bring in your own photos to show your family event and make a short PowerPoint presentation including the photos and a voice recording.

Materials to Bring

▶ Some pictures of your family event
▶ Electronic device(s) for making your PowerPoint presentation (e.g., laptop, tablet)

Grammar in Action

1. Particle 한테
2. Particle 한테서
3. Clausal connective –지만
4. Honorific expressions: Word level
5. Subject honorific suffix –(으)시–
6. Noun-modifying form for adjective (present) –(으)ㄴ

Step 1. [Planning] Recall the tasks in this chapter and plan your presentation. Don't forget to bring in materials in advance before performing the task. Think about how to organize the presentation of your memorable family event. Try to use the new grammar features in Chapter 1 when you plan your presentation.

Helpful questions to elicit the content of your presentation

▶ What kind of event did you attend?

▶ When and where was the event held?

▶ Who was with you at the event?

▶ What was at the event site? (e.g., 많은 음식이 있었어요.)

▶ What did you and other people (e.g., 부모님, 할아버지) do at the event?

▶ What was your opinion/impression of the event?

Step 2. [Rehearsing] Rehearse your presentation about the memorable family event. You can take notes to organize your presentation.

notes

Step 3. [Recording] **Make a short presentation using the pictures you brought and the information that you planned. Place your photos in the PowerPoint presentation coherently and record your voice while describing your family event (e.g., using the "Record Slide Show" function in PowerPoint).**

☞ Use the worksheet on page 203 to complete the task.

CHAPTER

02

Emails

Tasks

 Task 1
Request an Override in a Korean Class

 Task 2
Apply for a Korean Study Abroad Program

 Task 3
Present Study Abroad Program Experiences to Your Korean Professor

 Task 4
Real World Task: Write an Email to Your Korean Professor

Chapter Learning Outcomes

Students will be able to:

1. Write an email to make a request or report something they experienced

2. Use appropriate grammar forms to deliver the following functions:
   (1) Express their (or someone's) wish or desire
   (2) Organize and describe several events that take place chronologically and logically
   (3) Justify a position by providing proper background information
   (4) Describe objects that are involved in a current ongoing action

▶ **Expressing desire –고 싶다 and –고 싶어 하다**

☞ **–고 싶다 expresses the speaker's wish or desire.**
e.g., 저는 한국 친구를 <u>**만나고 싶어요.**</u>

☞ **–고 싶어 하다 expresses a wish or desire of someone other than the speaker.**
e.g., 민수는 한국어를 <u>**배우고 싶어 해요.**</u>

▶ **Clausal connective –어/아서**

☞ **Clausal connective –어/아서 links two clauses and indicates that the event or the state(s) in the second clause are the natural result of what is expressed in the first clause.**
e.g., 한국어가 <u>**재미있어서**</u> 한국어 수업을 들어요.

▶ **Clausal connective –(으)ㄴ/는데**

☞ **Clausal connective –(으)ㄴ/는데 is used to provide background information for the main clause.**
e.g., 지난 여름에 한국에 <u>**갔는데**</u> 너무 더웠어요.

▶ **Noun-modifying form for verb (present) –는**

☞ **The noun-modifying form –는 is used with a verb to modify a noun and indicates that the action is ongoing.**
e.g., 제가 <u>**좋아하는**</u> 한국 음식은 불고기하고 갈비입니다.

✓ Task Scenario

There are two sessions of Korean 201 this semester (9:00 AM and 2:00 PM). You want to take the 9:00 AM session with your friend, who wants to take the same course, but the class is full. So, you are writing an email to the Korean professor to request an override.

Grammar in Action

1. Expressing desire –고 싶다 and –고 싶어 하다
2. Clausal connective –어/아서
3. Clausal connective –(으)ㄴ/는데
4. Noun-modifying form for verb (present) –는

Helpful Words & Expressions

과목 subject	자주 often	쉽다 to be easy
굉장히 very much	전공 major	시작하다 to begin
교수님 professor	길이 막히다 to be blocked,	아르바이트하다 to do a
교통 transportation	congested	part-time job
기숙사 dormitory	놀다 to play, hang out	어렵다 to be difficult
다음 학기 next semester	늦다 to be late	여행하다 to travel
드라마 drama	다 차다 to be full	일하다 to work
룸메이트 roommate	배우다 to learn	(을/를) 잘하다 to be good at
멀리 far, far away	복잡하다 to be crowded	전공하다 to major in
문화 culture	불편하다 to be inconvenient,	졸업하다 to graduate
밖 outside	uncomfortable	죄송하다 to be sorry
연구실 professor's office	수업에 늦다 to be late for class	(하고) 이야기를 하다 to talk
이번 학기 this semester	수업을 듣다 to take a class	(with)
일찍 early	쉬다 to take a rest	

Self-introduction

▶ 저는 한국 문화를 **배우는** 학생이에요.

▶ I am a student who lives in a dorm with a Korean roommate.

▶ The courses that I'm taking this semester are _____.

▶ The subject that I major in is _____.

The reasons why you want to study Korean

▶ 저는 한국 드라마를 자주 **보는데** / 재미있어요.
　　(clause 1)　　　　　　　(clause 2)

▶ I have a Korean roommate / and I want to talk with him/her in Korean.
　　(clause 1)　　　　　　　　　　　(clause 2)

▶ _____ / _____.
　　　　(clause 1)　　　　　　　　　　(clause 2)

▶ _____ / _____.
　　　　(clause 1)　　　　　　　　　　(clause 2)

The reasons why you want to request an override into Korean 201 (9:00 AM session) this semester

▶ 저는 2시에 **일해서** / 2시 수업을 못 들어요.
　　(clause 1)　　　　　(clause 2)

▶ I will graduate next semester / so 이번 학기에 Korean 201 수업을 **듣고 싶어요**.
　　　(clause 1)　　　　　　　　　　　(clause 2)

▶ _____ / _____.
　　　　(clause 1)　　　　　　　　　　(clause 2)

▶ _____ / _____.
　　　　(clause 1)　　　　　　　　　　(clause 2)

notes

Step 2. [Writing] Write an email to your Korean professor to request an override into Korean 201.

☞ Use the worksheet on page 205 to complete the task.

✓ Task Scenario

You and your friend are planning to apply for a study abroad program to go to Korea together. You and your partner have information about two different programs (성실대학교 and 열정대학교). After sharing the program information, decide which program you and your partner will apply for. Based on your decision, you and your partner will write an email to the director of the Korean study abroad program to apply for the program.

Grammar in Action

1. **Expressing desire** –고 싶다 and –고 싶어 하다
2. **Clausal connective** –어/아서
3. **Clausal connective** –(으)ㄴ/는데
4. **Noun-modifying form for verb (present)** –는

Helpful Words & Expressions

가을 fall, autumn	안 inside	학비 tuition
과목 subject	언어 language	길이 막히다 to be blocked, congested
교수님 professor	역사 history	
교통 transportation	여름 summer	깨끗하다 to be clean
교환 exchange	연구실 professor's office	놀다 to play, hang out
국제 international	음악 music	늦다 to be late
굉장히 very much	자주 often	복잡하다 to be crowded
기간 period, term	장점 advantages	불편하다 to be inconvenient, uncomfortable
기숙사비 boarding expenses	전공 major	
단점 disadvantages	캠퍼스 campus	시작하다 to begin
룸메이트 roommate	케이팝 K-pop	연습하다 to practice
문화 culture	클럽 club	(에) 지원하다 to apply
메뉴 menu	프로그램 program	죄송하다 to be sorry
밖 outside	택시 taxi	편하다 to be convenient, comfortable
스터디 어브로드 study abroad	학기 semester	

Student A

Step 1. [Planning] Look at the information below. Come up with the missing information and think about how you are going to say the items in Korean. Try to use the new grammar features of Chapter 2. (You may change the order of the provided information and Korean expressions if needed.)

Information about study abroad program 1: 성실대학교

*These pictures are given to help you generate ideas. You may use these pictures to narrate a story.

▶ When: fall

▶ Program Information:
  • It is a very good school in Korea.
  • Transportation is very convenient.
  • <u>There are many classes that teach interesting Korean history.</u>

▶ Dormitory Information:
  성실대학교 캠퍼스 안에 있는 국제 기숙사
  • <u>미국 학생들과 같이 **사는** 기숙사예요.</u>
  • The dorm has a cafeteria with delicious Korean food.
  • Cost: $5,000

▶ **Tuition**: $33,000

Your motivation for studying abroad in Korea and your evaluation of the 성실대학교 program

Motivation for studying abroad in Korea

▶ 한국어를 잘 **못해서** 한국어를 **배우고 싶어요**.

▶ _____ / _____ .
  (clause 1)   (clause 2)

Advantages

▶ _____ .

▶ _____ .

Disadvantages

► _____.

► _____.

Step 2. [Sharing] **Exchange the information presented about advantages and disadvantages of the study abroad programs that you (성실대학교) and your partner (열정대학교) are considering. Then, decide which program you and your partner will apply for.**

► The program you and your partner will apply for together: _____

notes

Step 3. [Writing] **Write an email to the director of the Korean study abroad program to apply for the program.**

☞ Use the worksheet on page 209 to complete the task.

Student B

Step 1. [Planning] Look at the information below. Come up with the missing information and think about how you are going to say the items in Korean. Try to use the new grammar features of Chapter 2. (You may change the order of the provided information and Korean expressions if needed.)

Information about study abroad program 2: 열정대학교

*These pictures are given to help you generate ideas. You may use these pictures to narrate a story.

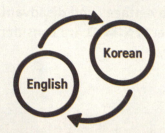

▶ When: summer

▶ Program Information:
  • It has good Korean classes.
  • 한국 문화를 **배우는** 클럽이 많아요.
  • It has a language exchange program in which you talk with Korean friends.

▶ Dormitory Information:
  열정대학교 캠퍼스 밖에 있는 기숙사
  • The dorm has clean rooms with big desks.
  • Students live with Korean students who like international students.
  • Cost: $1,500

▶ **Tuition**: $33,000

Your motivation for studying abroad in Korea and your evaluation of the 열정대학교 program

Motivation for studying abroad in Korea

▶ 케이팝을 **들었는데** 음악이 너무 좋았어요.

▶ _____ / _____ .
　　　　　　(clause 1)　　　　　　　　　　　　　　(clause 2)

Advantages

▶ _____

▶ _____

Disadvantages

► _____ .

► _____ .

Step 2. [Sharing] Exchange the information presented about advantages and disadvantages of the study abroad programs that you 열정대학교 and your partner 성실대학교 are considering. Then, decide which program you and your partner will apply for.

► The program you and your partner will apply for together: _____

notes

Step 3. [Writing] Write an email to the director of the Korean study abroad program to apply for the program.

☞ Use the worksheet on page 209 to complete the task.

Present Study Abroad Program Experiences to Your Korean Professor
Collaborative Speaking

 Task Scenario

You and your partner are currently studying abroad in Korea and are taking a Korean class during the study abroad program. One assignment that you and your partner have to complete together is to send a video message to your Korean professor back home about your study abroad experiences in Korea. In your video message, you will include four pictures you and your partner took during the study abroad program in Korea and describe each event.

Grammar in Action

1. **Expressing desire** –고 싶다 and –고 싶어 하다
2. **Clausal connective** –어/아서
3. **Clausal connective** –(으)ㄴ/는데
4. **Noun-modifying form for verb (present)** –는

Helpful Words & Expressions

과목 subject	숙제 homework	길이 막히다 to be blocked, congested
굉장히 very much	안 inside	
교수님 professor	언어 language	노래하다 sing a song
교통 transportation	역사 history	놀다 to play, to hang out
교환 exchange	자주 often	늦다 to be late
국제 international	장점 advantages	만들다 to make
김치 kimchi	전공 major	맵다 to be spicy
노래방 noraebang	제주도 Jeju Island	배우다 to learn
단점 disadvantages	차 tea	복잡하다 to be crowded
떡 rice cake	체험학습 field trip	불편하다 to be inconvenient, uncomfortable
룸메이트 roommate	캠퍼스 campus	
메뉴 menu	클럽 club	시작하다 to begin
문화 culture	프로그램 program	여행하다 to travel
밖 outside	택시 taxi	편하다 to be convenient, comfortable
비빔밥 bibimbap	가르치다 to teach	

Student A

Pictures of your friends that you took while studying abroad

The person who _____ is Linda.

_____을/를 **마시는** 사람은 사라 (Sarah)예요.

Good things

▶ I went shopping / and clothes were so cheap.
    (clause 1)   (clause 2)

▶ _____ / _____.
    (clause 1)   (clause 2)

Bad things

▶ 날씨가 너무 **더워서** / 조금 힘들었어요.
    (clause 1)   (clause 2)

▶ _____ / _____.
    (clause 1)   (clause 2)

*These pictures are given to help you generate ideas. You may use these pictures to narrate a story.

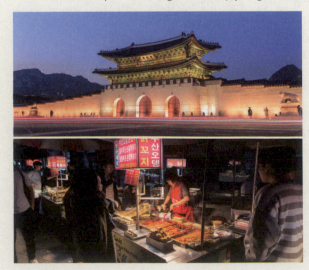

▶ 다음 주에 뭐 **하고 싶어요?**

• I want to meet my friend's grandmother who lives in Korea.

• _____ / _____ .
　　　　　　(clause 1)　　　　　　　　　　　　　　　　　　(clause 2)

Step 2. [Sharing/Rehearsing] **Using the information presented, share your study abroad experiences with you partner. Tell your partner the good things and bad things that you have experienced during the program. Then discuss what you and your partner want to do next week. After sharing the information, rehearse the video message collaboratively with your partner before recording.**

notes

_____

_____

_____

_____

_____

_____

Step 3. [Recording] **Record a video message for your Korean professor back home about the study abroad program.**

☞ Use the worksheet on page 213 to complete the task.

Student B

Step 1. [Planning] Look at the pictures that you took during your program. Come up with the missing information and think about how you are going to say the items in Korean. Try to use the new grammar features of Chapter 2. (You may change the order of the provided information and Korean expressions if needed.)

Pictures of your friends that you took during your study abroad

_____을/를 **먹는** 사람은 케이티 (Katie)예요.

The person who _____ is Mary.

Good things	Bad things

▶ **떡을 만들었는데** / 아주 맛있었어요.
    (clause 1)   (clause 2)

▶ _____ / _____.
    (clause 1)   (clause 2)

▶ I went on a field trip / and it was too far.
    (clause 1)   (clause 2)

▶ _____ / _____.
    (clause 1)   (clause 2)

*These pictures are given to help you generate ideas. You may use these pictures to narrate a story.

▶ 다음 주에 **뭐 하고 싶어요?**

- I want to go to a class where Professor Kim teaches Korean history.

- _____ / _____ .
  (clause 1)   (clause 2)

Step 2. [Sharing/Rehearsing] Using the information presented, share your study abroad experiences with you partner. Tell your partner the good things and bad things that you have experienced during the program. Then discuss what you and your partner want to do next week. After sharing the information, rehearse the video message collaboratively with your partner before recording.

notes

Step 3. [Recording] Record a video message for your Korean professor about the study abroad program.

☞ Use the worksheet on page 213 to complete the task.

✓ Task Scenario

You are going to write an email to your Korean professor about your Korean class. In your email, include why you are taking the Korean class, what you think about the class, and what you want to learn in class.

Grammar in Action

1. Expressing desire –고 싶다 and –고 싶어 하다
2. Clausal connective –어/아서
3. Clausal connective –(으)ㄴ/는데
4. Noun-modifying form for verb (present) –는

Helpful Words & Expressions

한국어를 배운 후에 after learning Korean

Step 1. [Planning] Recall the tasks in this chapter and plan your email. Think about how to organize your email. Try to use the new grammar features in Chapter 2 when you write your email.

Helpful questions to elicit the content of your email

▶ Why are you taking this Korean course?

▶ What do you want to do after learning Korean / taking this course?

▶ What do you like about the course?

▶ Is there anything that you want to do/learn in the course? Why?

▶ What suggestions do you have to improve the course?

▶ Is there anything that you want to say to the professor?

notes

Step 2. [Writing] Write an email to your Korean professor.

☞ Use the worksheet on page 215 to complete the task.

Text Messages

Tasks

Task 1
Text a Friend about Spring Break

Task 2
Text a Friend to Plan a Double Date

Task 3
Text a Friend to Plan a Study Session

Task 4
Real World Task: Text a Friend to Make Plans for the Weekend

Chapter Learning Outcomes

Students will be able to:
1. Exchange text messages with each other to plan personal events

2. Use appropriate grammar forms to deliver the following functions:
   (1) Express their current states of mind and activities
   (2) Express whether the quantity of an item is more (or less) than the speaker's expectations
   (3) Express a speaker's wish, desire, or intention
   (4) Make an informal suggestion or ask for a listener's opinion

Grammar Focus

▶ Progressive form –고 있다

☞ Progressive form –고 있다 is used with an action verb and indicates that an event is ongoing.

e.g., 미나가 민수하고 같이 테니스를 **치고 있어요.**

▶ Particles (이)나, 밖에

☞ Particle (이)나 is used with a noun and indicates that the noun exceeds the speaker's expectations.

e.g., 저는 어제 열 **시간이나** 잤어요.

☞ Particle 밖에 must appear with a negative form and indicates that the item or quantity in question is less than the speaker expected.

e.g., 저는 이번 학기에 두 **과목밖에** 안 들어요.

▶ Sentence ending –(으)ㄹ래요

☞ Sentence ending –(으)ㄹ래요 is used to express the speaker's wish, desire, or intention. It cannot be used with a third-person subject.

e.g., 저는 오늘 저녁에 한국 음식을 **먹을래요.**

☞ Sentence ending –(으)ㄹ래요 can be used as a suggestion if it is used in a question form.

e.g., 내일 저하고 영화 **볼래요?**

▶ Sentence ending –(으)ㄹ까요?

☞ Sentence ending –(으)ㄹ까요? is used to make an informal suggestion in a first-person (I, we) sentence.

e.g., 우리 같이 커피 **마실까요?**

☞ When sentence ending –(으)ㄹ까요? is used in a third-person (e.g., he, she, it, etc.) sentence, it asks for the listener's opinion.

e.g., 내일 비가 **올까요?**

▶ Particles A부터 B까지, A에서 B까지

☞ Particles A부터 B까지 are used with a temporal noun and indicates a range of time.

e.g., 저는 매일 오전 열 **시부터** 네 **시까지** 수업이 있어요.

☞ Particles A에서 B까지 are used with a spatial noun and indicate a range of the locations.

e.g., **집에서** **학교까지** 차로 30분쯤 걸려요.

Chapter 03
Task 1

Text a Friend about Spring Break

Collaborative Speaking & Writing

✅ Task Scenario

You and your partner are texting each other during your spring break. You and your partner are currently in different places (i.e., beach, Canada). You and your partner are talking about what you are doing with your family and trying to decide what you will do together at the end of your spring break when you return from your trip (i.e., the upcoming weekend).

Grammar in Action

1. Progressive form –고 있다
2. Particles (이)나, 밖에
3. Sentence ending –(으)ㄹ래요
4. Sentence ending –(으)ㄹ까요?
5. Particles A부터 B까지, A에서 B까지

Helpful Words & Expressions

가격 price
갈비 galbi
골프 golf
공원 park
날씨 weather
남동생 younger brother
달러 dollar
리조트 resort
바닷가 beach
보통 usually
봄방학 spring break
불고기 bulgogi
비행기 airplane

비행기표 airline ticket
여행 trip
연극 play
연극표 theater ticket
오늘 today
이번(에) this time
일요일 Sunday
캐나다 Canada
토요일 Saturday
호텔 hotel
걸리다 to take (time)
골프를 치다 to play golf
교회에 가다 to go to church

눈이 오다 to snow
돈이 들다 to cost
만들다 to make
바람이 불다 to be windy
비가 오다 to rain
사람이 많다 to be crowded
사진을 찍다 to take a picture
알아보다 to search for
요리하다 to cook
춤을 추다 to dance

Student A

Step 1. [Planning] Look at the following information about your spring break trip to the beach. Come up with the missing information and think about how you are going to say the items in Korean. Try to use the new grammar features of Chapter 3. (You may change the order of the provided information and Korean expressions if needed.)

Beach trip with your father

What you and your father are doing at a beach resort at the beach

[I]

?

_____.

[My father]

불고기를 **만들고 계세요.**

Weather

[Yesterday: Good]

_____.

[Now: It's raining]

_____.

How long did it take to get to the beach?

[Usually: 3 hours]

_____.

[Today: 6 hours (longer than expected)]

_____.

Are there many people?

[Usually: Crowded]

_____ .

[Today: Only 2 people]

사람이 두 **명밖에** 없어요.

Step 2. [Sharing] You want to meet with your partner during the upcoming weekend, when you return from your trip. Here is your current schedule. Considering your schedule, decide when and where to meet and what to do with your partner.

Time	Saturday	Sunday
2:00 pm		
3:00 pm	Playing golf with my younger brother	
4:00 pm		Going to a park to take pictures
5:00 pm		
6:00 pm		
7:00 pm		
8:00 pm		

notes

- -

- -

- -

- -

Step 3. [Writing] In pairs, write text messages in Korean about your spring break trip, and make a plan for the upcoming weekend.

☞ Use the worksheet on page 219 to complete the task.

Student B

Step 1. **[Planning]** Look at the following information about your spring break trip to Canada. Come up with the missing information and think about how you are going to say the items in Korean. Try to use the new grammar features of Chapter 3. (You may change the order of the provided information and Korean expressions if needed.)

Trip to Canada with your mother

What you and your mother are doing at the hotel

[I]

[My mother]

?

연극표를 **알아보고 있어요.**

_____.

Weather

[This morning: Windy]

_____.

[Now: It's snowing]

_____.

How long did it take to get to Canada?

[Usually: 2 hours]

2 hours

_____.

[Today: Only 1 hour and a half]

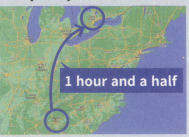

1 hour and a half

_____.

How much was the airline ticket?

[Usually: $350]

[This time: $500 (more expensive than expected)]

$350

$500

_____.

이번에 500**달러나** 들었어요.

Step 2. [Sharing] You want to meet with your partner during the upcoming weekend, when you return from your trip. Here is your current schedule. Considering your schedule, decide when and where to meet and what to do with your partner.

Time	Saturday	Sunday
2:00 pm		
3:00 pm		Going to church
4:00 pm		
5:00 pm		
6:00 pm	Going to dance at a dance class	
7:00 pm		
8:00 pm		

notes

....

....

....

....

Step 3. [Writing] In pairs, write text messages in Korean about your spring break trip, and make a plan for the upcoming weekend.

☞ Use the worksheet on page 219 to complete the task.

✅ Task Scenario

You and your friend are texting to plan a double date this weekend. You and your friend want to do one activity and then go to a restaurant afterwards together. While planning your double date, you will consider different factors, such as the weather, the location of the restaurant, and the types of food that you want to eat. Create text messages discussing the various factors and making a double date plan.

Grammar in Action

1. Progressive form –고 있다
2. Particles (이)나, 밖에
3. Sentence ending –(으)ㄹ래요
4. Sentence ending –(으)ㄹ까요?
5. Particles A부터 B까지, A에서 B까지

Helpful Words & Expressions

가격 price	영업시간 business hours	멀다 to be far
갈비 galbi	이번 주말 this weekend	문을 닫다 to close
거리 distance	일요일 Sunday	문을 열다 to open
계획 plan	일찍 early	비싸다 to be expensive
늦게 late	청바지 blue jeans	쉬다 to take a rest
닭갈비 chicken galbi	토요일 Saturday	시간이 많다
더블 데이트 double date	가깝다 to be near	to have a lot of time
맛 taste	눈이 오다 to snow	싸다 to be cheap
보통 usually	더블 데이트를 하다	(을/를) 잘하다 to be good at
삼겹살 pork belly	to double-date	할인하다 to give a discount
순두부 soft tofu	돈이 들다 to cost	
스포츠 sports	맵다 to be spicy	

Student A

Step 1. [Planning] Look at the information below. Come up with the missing information and think about how you are going to say the items in Korean. Try to use the new grammar features of Chapter 3. (You may change the order of the provided information and Korean expressions if needed.)

What you and your boyfriend are doing now

[I]

?

_____.

[My boyfriend]

청바지를 <u>**사고 있어요.**</u>

Different factors to consider & your suggestions

Weather during the weekend

[Saturday: It's snowing]

_____.

[Sunday: Good]

_____.

What you and your boyfriend like

(My boyfriend and I like sports.)

저하고 남자 친구는 _____.

Your suggestions

▶ 일요일에 시간이 많은데 우리 같이 일요일에 **만날까요?**

▶ And shall we _____?

Step 2. **[Sharing]** Share the information you have and decide what activity you and your partner want to do on the weekend.

Activity you and your partner will do together: _____

Also, discuss the two restaurant options below with your partner and decide which one you and your partner want to go to for dinner.

Restaurant options

What you want to ask your friend about the restaurants

▶ Distance: Korean BBQ가 **멀까요?** 순두부 식당이 **멀까요?**

▶ Business hours: _____? _____?

Your answers based on the information you have

▶ Price: 순두부 costs only $10, but Korean BBQ는 30**달러나** 들어요.

▶ Taste: _____ / _____.

                 (clause 1)   (clause 2)

notes

Step 3. [Writing] In pairs, write text messages in Korean to plan your weekend double date.

☞ Use the worksheet on page 223 to complete the task.

Student B

Step 1. [Planning] Look at the information below. Come up with the missing information and think about how you are going to say the items in Korean. Try to use the new grammar features of Chapter 3. (You may change the order of the provided information and Korean expressions if needed.)

What you and your girlfriend are doing now

[I]

?

_____

[My girlfriend]

is taking a rest

Different factors to consider & your suggestions

Information about the movie tickets for this weekend

[Usually: $20]

$20

_____

[This weekend: Only $10]

$10

10**달러밖에** 안 들어요!

What you and your girlfriend like

[My girlfriend and I like comedy movies.]

저하고 여자 친구는 _____.

Your suggestions

▶ 재미있는 영화가 있는데 우리 같이 극장에 **갈래요?**

▶ And would you like to _____?

Step 2. **[Sharing]** Share the information you have and decide what activity you and your partner want to do on the weekend.

Activity you and your partner will do together: _____

Also, discuss the two restaurant options below with your partner and decide which one you and your partner want to go to for dinner.

Restaurant options

What you want to ask your friend about the restaurants

▶ Price: Korean BBQ가 **쌀까요?** 순두부 식당이 **쌀까요?**

▶ Taste: _____ ? _____ ?

Your answer based on the information you have

▶ Distance: _____ / _____ .

▶ Business hours: Korean BBQ is open till 12 am, but 순두부 식당은 밤 11시까지 열어요.

notes
_____
_____
_____
_____
_____
_____
_____

Step 3. [Writing] In pairs, write text messages in Korean to plan your weekend double date.

☞ Use the worksheet on page 223 to complete the task.

Task Scenario

You and your partner are texting each other to check on how the semester is going. Next week is midterm week, and you and your partner are trying to set up a study session for tomorrow. In your texts, you will share information about your midterms and about tomorrow's schedule, and decide the time and location of your study session. Finally, you and your partner will discuss what you will do after midterm week.

Grammar in Action

1. Progressive form –고 있다
2. Particles (이)나, 밖에
3. Sentence ending –(으)ㄹ래요
4. Sentence ending –(으)ㄹ까요
5. Particles A부터 B까지, A에서 B까지

Helpful Words & Expressions

개 counting unit

거리 distance

기숙사 dormitory

닫는 시간 closing time

도서관 library

랩 lab

새벽 dawn

샌드위치 sandwich

생물학 biology

시험 exam

식물원 botanical garden

아침 식사 breakfast

어젯밤 last night

이번 학기 this semester

점심 lunch

중간고사 midterm

중간고사 기간 midterm week

지난 학기 last semester

커피숍 café

클럽 club

학기 semester

마시다 to drink

문을 닫다 to close

전화하다 to make a call

(을/를) 준비하다
   to prepare for

찾다 to look for

춤을 추다 to dance

Student A

Step 1. [Planning] Look at the information below. Come up with the missing information and think about how you are going to say the items in Korean. Try to use the new grammar features of Chapter 3. (You may change the order of the provided information and Korean expressions if needed.)

What are you doing now?

▶ 지금 점심을 _____.

Midterm schedule

[Last semester: Only 2 exams]

시험이 **2개밖에** 없었어요.

[This semester: 6 exams (more than expected)]

_____.

Your schedule for tomorrow

Time	Plan
9:00 am	Breakfast
10:00 am	Classes
11:00 am	
12:00 pm	
1:00 pm	Lunch
2:00 pm	First preferred time for the study session
3:00 pm	(*Suggest this option first!)
4:00 pm	
5:00 pm	Biology lab
6:00 pm	
7:00 pm	Second possible time for the study session
8:00 pm	

Location options for the study session

	School Library	Coffee Shop
Distance	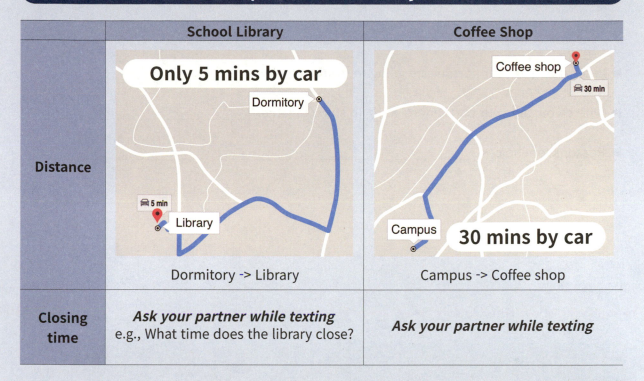 Only 5 mins by car — Dormitory, 🚗 5 min, Library / Dormitory -> Library	Coffee shop, 🚗 30 min, Campus, 30 mins by car / Campus -> Coffee shop
Closing time	***Ask your partner while texting*** e.g., What time does the library close?	***Ask your partner while texting***

What are you going to do after midterms?

(dance with friends)

▶ 시험이 끝나고 친구하고 클럽에 **갈래요.**

▶ And at the club _____.

▶ Reason (optional): _____.

Step 2. [Sharing] Share the information you have and decide when and where you and your partner want to study.

▶ When you and your partner are going to study together: _____

▶ Where you and your partner are going to study together: _____

▶ Reasons for choices: _____

notes

_____

_____

_____

_____

_____

_____

_____

_____

Step 3. [Writing] In pairs, write text messages in Korean to set up a study session for your midterm exams and to share what you want to do after exams.

☞ Use the worksheet on page 227 to complete the task.

Student B

Step 1. [Planning] Look at the information below. Come up with the missing information and think about how you are going to say the items in Korean. Try to use the new grammar features of Chapter 3. (You may change the order of the provided information and Korean expressions if needed.)

What are you doing now?

▶ 지금 도서관에서 책을 **찾고 있어요.**

Midterm schedule

[Last semester: 7 exams (more than expected)]

시험이 **7개나** 있었어요.

[This semester: Only 3 exams]

_____.

Your schedule for tomorrow

Time	Plan
9:00 am	Classes
10:00 am	
11:00 am	*Available for the study session*
12:00 pm	
1:00 pm	
2:00 pm	Classes
3:00 pm	
4:00 pm	Working in the lab
5:00 pm	
6:00 pm	
7:00 pm	*Available for the study session*
8:00 pm	

Location options for the study session

	School Library	Coffee Shop
Distance	*Ask your partner while texting* e.g., *how long does it take to get to the library?*	*Ask your partner while texting*
Closing time	10시까지 열어요	Open until 2:00 am

What are you going to do after midterms?

(walk at the botanical garden (식물원))

▶ 시험이 끝나고 친구하고 식물원에 **갈래요.**

▶ 그리고 식물원에서 _____.

▶ Reason (optional): _____.

Step 2. [Sharing] **Share the information you have and decide when and where you and your partner want to study.**

▶ When you and your partner are going to study together: _____

▶ Where you and your partner are going to study together: _____

▶ Reasons for choices: _____

notes

Step 3. [Writing] **In pairs, write text messages in Korean to set up a study session for your midterm exams and to share what you want to do after exams.**

☞ Use the worksheet on page 227 to complete the task.

Chapter 03
Task 4:
Real World Task

Text a Friend to Make Plans for the Weekend
Collaborative Writing

 **Task Scenario**

You are going to exchange text messages with your friend to make plans for the weekend. Discuss what you and your friend want to do together over the weekend and decide what activities you want to do and when and where to meet.

> ### Grammar in Action
>
> 1. Progressive form –고 있다
> 2. Particles (이)나, 밖에
> 3. Sentence ending –(으)ㄹ래요
> 4. Sentence ending –(으)ㄹ까요
> 5. Particles A부터 B까지, A에서 B까지

Step 1. [Planning] **Recall the tasks in this chapter and plan your text messages. Think about how to create text messages. Try to use the new grammar features of Chapter 3 when you write your text messages.**

Helpful topics to elicit the content of your text messages

▶ You can ask:

1. What your friend is doing

2. Your friend's weekend schedule

3. What your friend likes to do (e.g., activities, food)

▶ You can suggest:

1. A good restaurant including reasons

2. Fun activities (e.g., playing games or sports, watching a play or a movie)

Step 2. [Writing] In pairs, write text messages in Korean to make plans for the weekend. (Your instructor may also ask you to try this task using an application on your phone.)

☞ Use the worksheet on page 231 to complete the task.

04

Social Media Posts

Tasks

 Task 1
Write a Social Media Post about a Family Trip

 Task 2
Write a Social Media Post about Your High School Reunion

 Task 3
Post a Video on Social Media about Your High School Friends

 Task 4
Real World Task: Write a Social Media Post about a Memorable Event

Chapter Learning Outcomes

Students will be able to:
1. Post something they experienced on social media

2. Use appropriate grammar forms to deliver the following functions:
   (1) Organize and describe several events in sequential order
   (2) Describe a past event with proper elaboration
   (3) Describe someone's appearance in detail
       (e.g., what they are wearing, what color...)

Grammar Focus

▶ Clausal connective –어/아서

☞ **Clausal connective –어/아서 links two clauses and denotes the sequential occurrence of two related events. The event in the first clause functions as a precondition or manner of the following event.**
e.g., 지난 주말에 백화점에 **가서** 친구 선물을 샀어요.

▶ Noun-modifying form for verb (past) –(으)ㄴ

☞ **If noun-modifying form –(으)ㄴ is used with a verb, it modifies a noun and indicates that it is involved in a past event.**
e.g., 제가 어제 **만난** 친구는 제 고등학교 친구예요.

▶ ㅎ irregular

☞ **Some adjectives whose stem ends with ㅎ are conjugated irregularly. The ㅎ irregular adjectives are comprised of adjectives for five basic colors (빨갛다, 파랗다, 노랗다, 까맣다, 하얗다) and 어떻다, 이렇다, 그렇다 and 저렇다.**

☞ **When the stem is followed by the suffix that starts with 으, both ㅎ and 으 are omitted (e.g., 빨가면, 파란, 그런).**

☞ **When the stem is followed by the suffix that starts with 어/아, the vowel with the consonant ㅎ (i.e., 엏/앟) turns into the vowel "애" (e.g., 노래요, 이랬어요).**
e.g., 제 친구 생일 선물로 이 **빨간** 가방은 어때요?

▶ 'Wearing' verbs

☞ **The Korean language has different verbs for the English verb 'wear' based on the types of items (e.g., clothes, shoes, hat, and accessories):**
입다: 옷, 바지, 치마, 셔츠, 코트
신다: 신발, 양말
쓰다: 모자, 안경
끼다: 반지, 장갑, 안경
하다: 귀걸이, 목걸이, 넥타이, 벨트
차다: 시계, 팔찌
매다: 넥타이
메다: 가방

Chapter 04
Task 1

Write a Social Media Post about a Family Trip
Individual Writing

 Task Scenario

You and your family went on a trip to Los Angeles. You visited Santa Monica Beach on Day 1 and went to Disneyland on Day 2. You are going to write a social media post using pictures to introduce your family members and share information about your family trip.

Grammar in Action

1. Clausal connective –어/아서
2. Noun-modifying form for verb (past) –(으)ㄴ
3. ㅎ irregular
4. 'Wearing' verbs

Helpful Words & Expressions

꽃 flower
디즈니랜드 Disneyland
로스 앤젤레스 Los Angeles
모래성 sandcastle
미니 Minnie Mouse
미키 Mickey Mouse
바닷가 beach
반지 ring
백화점 department store
선글라스 sunglasses
셔츠 shirts
안경 glasses

여행 trip
할리우드 Hollywood
헤어밴드 hairband
호텔 hotel
까맣다 to be black
끼다 to wear (a ring, gloves, glasses)
노랗다 to be yellow
만나다 to meet
매다 to wear (a necktie)
빨갛다 to be red
사다 to buy

사진을 찍다 to take a picture
쓰다 to wear (a hat, glasses)
앉다 to sit
일어나다 to wake up
입다 to wear (clothes)
파랗다 to be blue
하얗다 to be white

Day 1 (morning): What you and your family did in Hollywood together

Black shirt

▶ 아침에 **일어나서** / _____.

    (clause 1)   (clause 2)

▶ The shirt that I _____ at the department store was black.

Day 1 (afternoon): What Santa Monica Beach was like & What your family did there

▶ Sandcastle that _____ was white.

▶ The beach was blue / _____.
   (clause 1)   (clause 2)

할머니

 → **?**

▶ My grandmother went to the hotel / and then _____.
   (clause 1)   (clause 2)

I (나)

 → **?**

Sit

▶ 바닷가에 **앉아서** / and then _____.
   (clause 1)   (clause 2)

▶ The flowers were red / so _____.
    (clause 1)   (clause 2)

▶ 선글라스를 **쓰고** _____ 반지를 _____ 사람은 제 누나/언니예요.

My mother

▶ _____ / and then _____.
         (clause 1)   (clause 2)

My younger brother

▶ _____ / and then _____.
         (clause 1)   (clause 2)

Step 2. [Writing] Write a social media post to share your family trip and make comments on other people's posts about their family trip.

☞ Use the worksheet on page 235 to complete the task.

Task Scenario

You and your friend graduated from the same high school and had a high school reunion in New York City last winter break. You and your partner met different friends at the high school reunion. You are going to write a post on a social media group page (for your high school reunion) to introduce your friends in the picture and describe what they have been doing since graduation.

Grammar in Action

1. Clausal connective –어/아서
2. Noun-modifying form for verb (past) –(으)ㄴ
3. ㅎ irregular
4. 'Wearing' verbs

Helpful Words & Expressions

가게 store	시카고 Chicago	만들다 to make
가방 bag	안경 glasses	매다 to wear (a necktie)
고등학교 high school	영국 England	빨갛다 to be red
곳 place	장갑 gloves	사다 to buy
귀걸이 earring	장소 place	쇼핑하다 to go shopping
그때 at that time	치마 skirt	쓰다 to use, write, wear
넥타이 necktie	크리스마스 트리 Christmas tree	(a hat, glasses)
뉴욕 New York	티셔츠 T-shirts	요리하다 to cook
도시 city	회색 gray	이사하다 to move (to a
동창회 reunion	가다 to go	different place)
모자 cap, hat	결혼하다 to marry	입다 to wear (clothes)
목걸이 necklace	까맣다 to be black	차다 to wear (a belt)
바지 pants	끝나다 to end	파랗다 to be blue
반지 rings	끼다 to wear (a ring, gloves,	하다 to wear (a necktie,
산타클로스 Santa Claus	glasses)	accessories)
센트럴파크 Central Park	노랗다 to be yellow	하얗다 to be white
셔츠 shirts	눈이 오다 to snow	
시계 watch, clock	만나다 to meet	

Student A

The person whom I met at the high school reunion

스티브
(Steve)

▶ **빨간** 모자를 **쓰고** _____ 안경을 _____ 사람이 스티브예요.

▶ 스티브는 영국에 **가서** _____.
　　　　(clause 1)　　　　　　　　　　　　　(clause 2)

What we did at the high school reunion

▶ I was wearing a/an _____ belt at that time.

▶ We _____ / and then ate it together.
　　(clause 1)　　　　　　　　　　(clause 2)

▶ The food that we _____ was delicious.

▶ The place where we _____ was New York.

▶ It was snowing a lot / so _____.
　　　　　(clause 1)　　　　　　　　　(clause 2)

▶ We went to Central Park / and then _____.
　　　　　(clause 1)　　　　　　　　　　(clause 2)

Step 2. [Sharing] You and your partner met different friends at the high school reunion. Using the information presented, introduce your friends in the picture to your partner and describe what they have been doing since graduation.

notes

_____

Step 3. [Writing] In pairs, write a post about your friends and make two comments on your friends' posts in the high school reunion social media group.

☞ Use the worksheet on page 239 to complete the task.

Student B

Step 1. [Planning] Look at the information below. Come up with the missing information and think about how you are going to say the items in Korean. Try to use the new grammar features of Chapter 4. (You may change the order of the provided information and Korean expressions if needed.)

The person whom I met at the high school reunion

잭
(Jack)

▶ The person who is wearing a white shirt and

_____ is Jack.

▶ 잭은 시카고로 **이사해서** / _____.

    (clause 1)   (clause 2)

What we did at the high school reunion

▶ I was wearing a/an _____ ring at that time.

▶ I _____ / and then gave it to my friend.

    (clause 1)   (clause 2)

▶ The letter that I _____ was so pretty.

▶ We met Santa Claus /

    (clause 1)

and then _____ (with Santa).

            (clause 2)

▶ 산타클로스가 저희한테 **준** 선물은 예쁜 크리스마스 카드였어요.

▶ 동창회가 끝나고 뉴욕에서 쇼핑을 했어요.

I bought a bag at the store / and the bag was _____.

    (clause 1)   (clause 2)

Step 2. [Sharing] You and your partner met different friends at the high school reunion. Using the information presented, introduce your friends in the picture to your partner and describe what they have been doing since graduation.

notes

Step 3. [Writing] In pairs, write a post about your friends and make two comments on your friends' posts in the high school reunion social media group.

☞ Use the worksheet on page 239 to complete the task.

Post a Video on Social Media about Your High School Friends

Individual Speaking

✅ Task Scenario

You went to a high school reunion last week. Now, you are making a video to upload on the social media group page of your high school reunion. In the video, you are introducing your friends and describing what they have been doing since graduation using a picture that you took at the reunion as the beginning of the video.

Grammar in Action

1. Clausal connective –어/아서
2. Noun-modifying form for verb (past) –(으)ㄴ
3. ㅎ irregular
4. 'Wearing' verbs

Helpful Words & Expressions

귀걸이 earring
넥타이 necktie
동창회 reunion
모자 cap, hat
목걸이 necklace
바지 pants
반지 rings
셔츠 shirts
선글라스 sunglasses
시계 watch, clock
시카고 Chicago
안경 glasses
액세서리 accessories
여자친구 girlfriend

장갑 gloves
치마 skirt
티셔츠 T-shirts
회색 gray
가다 to go
결혼하다 to marry
까맣다 to be black
끼다 to wear (a ring, gloves, glasses)
노랗다 to be yellow
만나다 to meet
만들다 to make
매다 to wear (a necktie)
빨갛다 to be red

사다 to buy
쓰다 to use, write, wear (a hat, glasses)
입다 to wear (clothes)
졸업하다 to graduate
파랗다 to be blue
하다 to wear (a necktie, accessories)
하얗다 to be white

	Clothes	Accessories	What did they / you do after graduation?
Steve (스티브)		모자	여자 친구하고 **결혼해서** / _____. (clause 1)　　　　　　　　　(clause 2)
Mina (미나)		선글라스	졸업하고 시카고로 **가서** / _____. (clause 1)　　　　　　　　　(clause 2)
Linda (린다)			_____ / and then _____. (clause 1)　　　　　　　　　(clause 2)
I			_____ / and then _____. (clause 1)　　　　　　　　　(clause 2)

Step 2. [Rehearsing] **Rehearse your video recording about the high school reunion, using the information presented. You can take notes to organize your video.**

Helpful information to elicit the content of your video

1. Greetings
2. Description of the high school reunion and yourself
3. Introduction of at least three friends from the picture
   · Description of their clothes and accessories including color
   · Description of their experiences, focusing on what they have been doing since high school graduation
4. Closing remark:
   "다음은 우리가 같이 **한** 액티비티를 얘기할 거예요."

notes
_____
_____
_____
_____
_____

Step 3. [Recording] **Record your video using the notes above.**

☞ Use the worksheet on page 243 to complete the task.

Chapter 04
Task 4:
Real World Task

Write a Social Media Post about a Memorable Event
Individual Writing

✓ Task Scenario

Write a social media post about a memorable past event in which you participated.

Materials to Bring

▶ Some pictures of your memorable event

Grammar in Action

1. Clausal connective –어/아서
2. Noun-modifying form for verb (past) –(으)ㄴ
3. ㅎ irregular
4. 'Wearing' verbs

Step 1. [Planning] Recall the tasks in this chapter and plan your social media post. Don't forget to bring some pictures in advance before performing the task. Think about how to organize the description of your memorable event. Try to use the new grammar features of Chapter 4 when you write your post.

Helpful questions to elicit the content of your post

▶ What event did you participate in?

▶ Who was at the event?

▶ What did they wear?

▶ What were they doing during the event?

▶ What have they been doing since then?

▶ How did you feel about the event?

notes

Step 2. [Writing] Write a social media post about your memorable event based on your picture(s) and the information prepared.

☞ Use the worksheet on page 245 to complete the task.

CHAPTER

05

Phone Conversations

Tasks

 Task 1
Talk on the Phone to Plan Korean Cultural Festival Events

 Task 2
Talk on the Phone to Discuss Changing a Presentation Date

 Task 3
Leave a Voicemail Message to Request a Change in
Presentation Date

 Task 4
Real World Task: Leave a Voicemail Message for Your
Korean Professor

Chapter Learning Outcomes

Students will be able to:

1. Communicate via phone to plan an event or make a request

2. Use appropriate grammar forms to complete the
   following functions:
   (1) Indicate the beneficiary of an action
   (2) Provide a reason for or cause of an action
   (3) Express that it is very important or necessary
       for something to happen
   (4) Express a wish, desire, or intention

Grammar Focus

▶ **Benefactive expression –어/아 주다**

☞ The auxiliary verb **–어/아 주다** expresses that the subject does something for the benefit of someone else.
e.g., 친구가 나한테 생일 선물을 **사 줬어요.**

▶ **Expressing obligation or necessity –어/아야 되다/하다**

☞ The auxiliary verb **–어/아야 되다/하다** indicates obligation or necessity.
It indicates the speaker's attitude or perspective that it is very important or necessary for something to happen.
e.g., 한국어 시험 때문에 오늘은 도서관에서 **공부해야 돼요/해요.**

▶ **Causal expression Noun 때문에**

☞ If a noun is used with **때문에**, it indicates that the noun is the reason or cause.
e.g., **시험 때문에** 잠을 못 잤어요.

▶ **Intentional –(으)ㄹ게요**

☞ The sentence ender **–(으)ㄹ게요** is used with the first person (I, we) and indicates that the speaker is promising or offering to perform an action in the immediate future.
e.g., 오늘은 제가 요리를 **할게요.**

▶ **Intentional –겠–**

☞ The suffix **–겠–** is used with the first person (I, we) and indicates the speaker is promising or offering to perform a task. Unlike **–(으)ㄹ게요**, **–겠–** can be used with the deferential ending **–(스)ㅂ니다.**
e.g., 내일 다시 **오겠습니다.**

Chapter 05
Task 1

Talk on the Phone to Plan Korean Cultural Festival Events
Collaborative Speaking

 Task Scenario

You are the president of the Korean Culture Club, and your partner is the treasurer of the club. You and your partner are trying to change the site of and raise funds for the festival. After discussing on the phone what you plan to do during the festival, decide the date when you and your partner will visit the festival organizer to get advice on festival planning, who will buy the gifts for student participants, who will borrow hanbok (Korean traditional clothes) and instruments, and who will prepare the ingredients for the Korean food.

Grammar in Action

1. Benefactive expression –어/아 주다
2. Expressing obligation or necessity –어/아야 되다/하다
3. Causal expression Noun 때문에
4. Intentional –(으)ㄹ게요
5. Intentional –겠–

Helpful Words & Expressions

글씨 handwriting
돈 money
동안 during, for
면담 시간 office hours
물가 cost of living
스케줄 schedule
악기 instrument
운동장 stadium
이벤트 event
이유 reason
인터뷰 interview
장소 place

재료 ingredient
조 모임 group meeting
주최자 organizer
축제 festival
춤 dance
포스터 poster
학생회관 student center
한복 hanbok (Korean traditional clothes)
회계 treasurer
회장 president (of a club)
꾸미다 to decorate

바꾸다 to change
보내다 to send
뵙다 to see (honorific)
붙이다 to put (a poster) on
빌려주다 to lend
빌리다 to borrow
소개하다 to introduce
(을/를) 준비하다 to prepare
(이/가) 필요하다 to be necessary

Student A

Step 1. [Planning] Look at the information below. Come up with the missing information and think about how you are going to say the items in Korean. Try to use the new grammar features of Chapter 5. (You may change the order of the provided information and Korean expressions if needed.)

Event ideas that you want to include in the Korean cultural festival

*These pictures are given to help you generate ideas. You may use these pictures to narrate a story.

_____

Teach K-pop dance to students

What you have to do for the festival

▶ 포스터를 **붙여야 돼요**.

▶ _____.

▶ _____.

Reasons why the club has to change the festival site from 운동장 to 학생회관

▶ We have to change the site because of possible bad weather.

▶ _____.

Step 2. [Sharing/Rehearsing] Share why you want to change the site and raise funds with your partner as if you and your partner were talking on the phone. Decide the following: when you and your partner will visit the festival organizer (김 선생님) based on the following schedule, who will buy the gifts for student participants, who will borrow hanbok and instruments, and who will prepare the ingredients for the Korean food. After sharing the information, rehearse the phone conversation collaboratively with your partner before recording.

✓ **김 선생님 면담 시간 (office hours): 화, 수, 목 오후 2:00 - 4:30**

✓ **내 스케줄**

월요일	화요일	수요일	목요일	금요일
	1:00-3:00 PM 랩 - 3:00-5:00 PM 조 모임	12:00-2:00 PM 생물학 수업	김 선생님을 뵙고 싶은 날	

▶ 같이 김 선생님을 뵙고 싶은 요일하고 시간: _____

▶ 선물을 사는 사람: _____

▶ 한복하고 악기를 빌리는 사람: _____

▶ 한국 음식 재료를 준비하는 사람: _____

notes

Step 3. [Recording] Record your conversation as if you and your partner were talking on the phone discussing the Korean cultural festival.

☞ Use the worksheet on page 249 to complete the task.

Student B

Event ideas that you want to include in the Korean cultural festival

*These pictures are given to help you generate ideas. You may use these pictures to narrate a story.

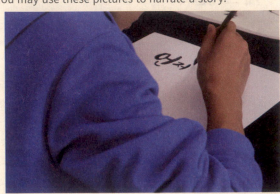

학생들한테 한 시간 동안 한복을 **빌려줘요.**

_____.

What you have to do for the event

▶ I have to send an email to the students.

▶ _____.

▶ _____.

Reasons why the club needs more money

▶ 비싼 **물가 때문에** 돈이 더 **있어야 돼요.**

▶ _____.

[Sharing/Rehearsing] Share why you want to change the site and raise funds with your partner as if you and your partner were talking on the phone. Decide the following: when you and your partner will visit the festival organizer (김 선생님) based on the following schedule, who will buy the gifts for student participants, who will borrow hanbok and instruments, and who will prepare the ingredients for the Korean food. After sharing the information, rehearse the phone conversation collaboratively with your partner before recording.

✔ **김 선생님 면담 시간 (office hours):** 화, 수, 목 오후 2:00 - 4:30
✔ **내 스케줄**

월요일	화요일	수요일	목요일	금요일
	김 선생님을 뵙고 싶은 날	5:00-7:00 PM 경제학 수업	1:00-3:00 PM 인터뷰 준비 - 3:00-5:00 PM 인터뷰	

▶ 같이 김 선생님을 뵙고 싶은 요일하고 시간: _____

▶ 선물을 사는 사람: _____

▶ 한복하고 악기를 빌리는 사람: _____

▶ 한국 음식 재료를 준비하는 사람: _____

notes

Step 3. [Recording] Record your conversation as if you and your partner were talking on the phone discussing the Korean cultural festival.

☞ Use the worksheet on page 249 to complete the task.

Chapter 05
Task 2

Talk on the Phone to Discuss Changing a Presentation Date
Collaborative Speaking

 Task Scenario

You and your partner are working on a group project in a Korean class. Your group presentation is scheduled for next Monday, but your group wants to change the presentation date for several reasons. To ask your professor to change the date, you and your partner need to first discuss an alternative date for the presentation, who is going to call the professor on the phone, and who is taking charge of preparing the PowerPoint and other presentation materials.

Grammar in Action

1. Benefactive expression –어/아 주다
2. Expressing obligation or necessity –어/아야 되다/하다
3. Causal expression Noun 때문에
4. Intentional –(으)ㄹ게요
5. Intentional –겠–

Helpful Words & Expressions

감기 cold (noun)
결혼식 wedding ceremony
결혼 축하 파티 wedding
    reception
교수님 professor
댁 house (honorific)
룸메이트 roommate
머리 head, hair
목 neck, throat
발표 presentation
부모님 parents

사진 picture
아직 yet, still
약 medicine, drugs
오빠 older brother
    (of a female speaker)
이유 reason
인터뷰 interview
인턴십 internship
자료 materials
집 house
파워포인트 PowerPoint

형 older brother
    (of a male speaker)
감기에 걸리다 to catch a cold
결혼하다 to marry
낫다 to recover
돕다 to help
아프다 to be sick
사진을 찍다 to take
    (a picture)
춥다 to be cold

Student A

Why you cannot do your presentation on the scheduled date

▶ Reason: Your brother is having his wedding reception at your parents' house.

[Because of brother's wedding]　　　　　[Have to go to my parents' house]

　　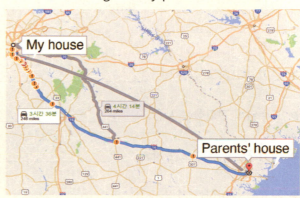

▶ Things that you want to do for your brother at the reception

• 결혼 파티에서 형의 사진을 **찍어 주고** 싶어요.

• _____.

▶ Things that you have to do at the reception

• 결혼 파티 준비를 **도와야 돼요**.

• _____.

Step 2. [Sharing/Rehearsing] Exchange the reasons why you need to change your presentation date with your partner. Decide when you and your partner would like to do the presentation, who will call the professor, and who will prepare the PowerPoint and other presentation materials. After sharing the information, rehearse the phone conversation collaboratively with your partner before recording.

	Mon	Tue	Wed	Thu	Fri	Sat	Sun
This Week				Today			Brother's Wedding
Next Week	Presentation	Preferred date		Very difficult test			

▶ 같이 발표하고 싶은 날: _____

▶ 교수님께 전화하는 사람: _____

▶ 파워포인트를 만드는 사람: _____

▶ 자료를 준비하는 사람: _____

notes

Step 3. [Recording] Record your conversation as if you and your partner were talking on the phone discussing the presentation schedule.

☞ Use the worksheet on page 251 to complete the task.

Student B

Step 1. [Planning] Look at the information below. Come up with the missing information and think about how you are going to say the items in Korean. Try to use the new grammar features of Chapter 5. (You may change the order of the provided information and Korean expressions if needed.)

Why you cannot do your presentation on the scheduled date

▶ Reason: You have a cold.

[추운 **날씨 때문에**]　　　　　　　　　　　　　　　　[a cold]

▶ What your roommate did *for* you

- 룸메이트가 저한테 약을 **사 줬어요**.

- 그리고 룸메이트가 _____.

- However, I still have a headache, and my throat hurts.

▶ 낫기 위해서(to recover), what you must do

- I have to sleep a lot.

- _____

Exchange the reasons why you need to change your presentation date with your partner. Decide when you and your partner would like to do the presentation, who will call the professor, and who will prepare the PowerPoint and other presentation materials. After sharing the information, rehearse the phone conversation collaboratively with your partner before recording.

	Mon	Tue	Wed	Thu	Fri	Sat	Sun
This Week			Got a cold	**Today**			
Next Week	**Presentation**	Interview		**Preferred date**			

▶ 같이 발표하고 싶은 날: _____

▶ 교수님께 전화하는 사람: _____

▶ 파워포인트를 만드는 사람: _____

▶ 자료를 준비하는 사람: _____

notes
_____
_____
_____

Step 3. [Recording] Record your conversation as if you and your partner were talking on the phone discussing the presentation schedule.

☞ Use the worksheet on page 251 to complete the task.

Chapter 05
Task 3

Leave a Voicemail Message to Request a Change in Presentation Date
Individual Speaking (Prerequisite: Chapter 05, Task 2)

 Task Scenario

You just talked with your partner on the phone about changing the date of your presentation for your Korean course project. You discussed the reasons why you and your partner want to change the date, an alternative date for the presentation, who is going to call the professor to request the change, and who is taking charge of preparing the PowerPoint and other presentation materials. It was decided that you were going to call the professor, so you did, but the professor didn't answer the phone. So, you are leaving a voicemail message about changing the presentation date.

Grammar in Action

1. Benefactive expression –어/아 주다
2. Expressing obligation or necessity –어/아야 되다/하다
3. Causal expression Noun 때문에
4. Intentional –(으)ㄹ게요
5. Intentional –겠–

Helpful Words & Expressions

감기 cold (noun)
결혼식 wedding ceremony
결혼 축하 파티 wedding
　　reception
교수님 professor
댁 house (honorific)
룸메이트 roommate
머리 head, hair
목 neck, throat
발표 presentation
부모님 parents

사진 picture
아직 yet, still
약 medicine, drugs
오빠 older brother
　　(of a female speaker)
이유 reason
인터뷰 interview
인턴십 internship
자료 materials
집 house
파워포인트 PowerPoint

형 older brother
　　(of a male speaker)
감기에 걸리다 to catch a cold
결혼하다 to marry
낫다 to recover
돕다 to help
아프다 to be sick
사진을 찍다 to take
　　(a picture)
춥다 to be cold

Step 1. [Planning] Look at the information below. Come up with the missing information and think about how you are going to say the items in Korean. Try to use the new grammar features of Chapter 5. (You may change the order of the provided information and Korean expressions if needed.)

Why you / your partner cannot do a presentation on the scheduled date

* If you were Student A in Task 2, the information below is about you. If you were Student B in Task 2, the information is about your partner. Modify the provided information according to your role in Task 2.

▶ Reason: Your brother will have his wedding reception at your parents' house.

[Because of brother's wedding]   [Have to go to my parents' house]

   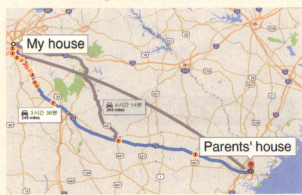

▶ Things that you want to do for your brother at the reception

- 결혼 파티에서 형의 사진을 **찍어 주고** 싶어요.

- _____.

▶ Things that you have to do at the reception

- 결혼 파티 준비를 **도와야 돼요.**

- _____.

Why you / your partner cannot do a presentation on the scheduled date

* If you were Student A in Task 2, the information below is about your partner. If you were Student B in Task 2, the information is about you. Modify the provided information according to your role in Task 2.

▶ Reason: You have a cold.

[추운 **날씨 때문에**]   [a cold]

▶ What your roommate did *for* you

• 룸메이트가 저한테 약을 **사 줬어요**.

• 그리고 룸메이트가 _____.

• However, I still have a headache, and my throat hurts.

▶ 낫기 위해서(to recover), what you must do

• I have to sleep a lot.

• _____.

▶ 같이 발표하고 싶은 날: _____

▶ 파워포인트를 만드는 사람: _____

▶ 자료를 준비하는 사람: _____

Step 2. [Rehearsing] Rehearse your voicemail message about changing the presentation date using the information presented.

Helpful information to elicit the content of your voicemail message

1. Greeting on the phone
2. Why you are calling
3. Asking the professor to change the presentation date
4. All the reasons why you and your partner cannot meet the presentation date with detailed information
5. Suggesting the date when you and your partner want to do the presentation
6. Two closing sentences that indicate that you and your partner will send the PowerPoint slides via email and that you and your partner will work hard
7. Closing on the phone: "그럼, 나중에 다시 전화 **드리겠습니다.**"

notes

_____

_____

_____

_____

_____

_____

_____

_____

_____

_____

_____

Step 3. [Recording] **Record your voicemail message using the notes you prepared.**

☞ Use the worksheet on page 253 to complete the task.

Chapter 05
Task 4:
Real World Task

Leave a Voicemail Message for Your Korean Professor
Individual Speaking

 Task Scenario

Leave a voicemail message for your Korean professor to request if you can change the date and time of your final exam and make an appointment to visit your professor's office to talk about your request/suggestion.

Grammar in Action

1. Benefactive expression –어/아 주다
2. Expressing obligation or necessity –어/아야 되다/하다
3. Causal expression Noun 때문에
4. Intentional –(으)ㄹ게요
5. Intentional –겠–

Step 1. [Planning] Recall the tasks in this chapter and plan your voicemail message. Think about how to organize your voicemail message. Try to use the new grammar features of Chapter 5 when you plan your voicemail message.

Helpful questions to elicit the content of your voicemail message

1. Why are you calling?

2. What do you want to talk about with your professor?

3. Why do you want to change the final exam date and time?

   Try to think about logical reasons for your request.

4. When do you want to meet your professor?

   Suggest your preferred time for a visit. Think about your professor's office hours.

5. What other suggestions/requests would you like to make of your professor?

   Include at least one more suggestion/request for your professor to benefit your Korean studies.

Step 2. [Rehearsing] Rehearse the voicemail message that you planned. You can take notes to organize your message.

notes

Step 3. [Recording] Record your voicemail message using the the information prepared. Record your voicemail message with your phone and send it to your professor.

☞ Use the worksheet on page 255 to complete the task.

Postcards

Tasks

 Task 1
Write a Postcard to Your Friend while Studying in Korea

 Task 2
Write a Postcard to a Friend You Met during Study Abroad in Korea

 Task 3
Send a Video Message to a Friend You Met during Study Abroad in Korea

 Task 4
Real World Task: Send a Postcard to Your Friend

Chapter Learning Outcomes

Students will be able to:

1. Send a message on a postcard or in video format to report their experiences or to give advice to someone

2. Use appropriate grammar forms to complete the following functions:
   (1) Provide a reason for or describe the cause of an action
   (2) Express what they cannot do and provide a suitable reason
   (3) Give a suggestion or advice on what cannot be done in a certain situation with proper justification
   (4) Describe a situation or status in elaborate ways

Grammar Focus

▶ **Causal expression Noun(이)라서**

☞ **Causal expression Noun(이)라서 is the combination of clausal connective –어/아서 and the main verb –이다 (to be) and denotes "because someone/ something is noun."**
e.g., **여름이라서** 날씨가 더워요.

▶ **Negative expression –지 못하다**

☞ **If negative expression form –지 못하다 is used with a verb, it implies that a situation is outside the speaker's control.**
e.g., 다음 주에 한국어 시험이 있어서 주말에 파티에 **가지 못해요.**

▶ **Negative command –지 말다**

☞ **If negative command –지 말다 is used with a verb, it implies the prohibition of an action.**
e.g., 수업 시간에 핸드폰을 **하지 마세요.**

▶ **Adverbial suffix –게**

☞ **The adverbial suffix –게 is attached to an adjective stem to indicate the manner or way in which something happens.**
e.g., 어제 친구하고 같이 파티에서 **재미있게** 놀았어요.

▶ **르 irregular**

☞ **Some verbs and adjectives whose stem ends with 르 are conjugated irregularly. When the stem is followed by a suffix that starts with 어/아, the vowel 으 in the stem is omitted and ㄹ is added to the 받침 of the previous syllable (e.g., 불러요, 빨라서, 몰랐어요).**
e.g., 제 친구는 노래를 정말 잘 **불러요.**

▶ **Clausal connective –(으)니까**

☞ **Clausal connective –(으)니까 is used to express the reason or justification for the event or states in the second clause. Unlike –어/아서, it can be used as a justification for the speaker's suggestion or prohibition.**
e.g., 비가 **오니까** 우산을 가져 가세요.

Chapter 06
Task 1

Write a Postcard to Your Friend while Studying in Korea
Collaborative Speaking & Writing

✓ Task Scenario

You and your partner are participating in a study abroad program in Korea now. You are writing a postcard to 스티브, a student who will come to Seoul, Korea, for study abroad next semester. In the postcard, you and your partner share what Seoul is like, how you have been doing lately, and what you have liked about your study abroad program. Also, give some tips about Korean culture to 스티브.

Grammar in Action

1. Causal expression Noun(이)라서
2. Negative expression –지 못하다
3. Negative command –지 말다
4. Adverbial suffix –게
5. 르 irregular
6. Clausal connective –(으)니까

Helpful Words & Expressions

공원 park	신발 shoes	덥다 to be hot
교실 classroom	안 inside	모자를 쓰다 to wear a cap
노래 song	여름 summer	바쁘다 to be busy
대학교 university	제주도 Jeju Island	빠르다 to be fast
도시 city	지금 now	사다 to buy
룸메이트 roommate	지하철 subway	살다 to live
모자 cap, hat	콘서트 concert	신발을 신다 to wear shoes
문화 culture	택시 기사 taxi driver	여행하다 to travel
사물놀이 samullori (traditional Korean instrumental music)	팁 tip	재미있다 to be fun
	표 ticket	주다 to give
	프랑스 France	즐겁다 to be joyful
서울 Seoul	가르치다 to teach	지내다 to spend (time), live
수업 class, lesson	노래를 부르다 to sing a song	행복하다 to be happy
숙제 homework	(하고) 다르다 to be different	

Step 1. [Planning] Look at the information below. Come up with the missing information and think about how you are going to say the items in Korean. Try to use the new grammar features of Chapter 6. (You may change the order of the provided information and Korean expressions if needed.)

My life in Seoul

[cause] → [effect]

▶ 서울은 지금 **여름이라서** / _____ .
   (clause 1)   (clause 2)

▶ 저는 한국에서 **행복하게** 지내고 있어요.

▶ 한국에서 친구들하고 _____ 지내고 있어요.

My life during study abroad

→ ?

▶ Roommate is French.

▶ The culture is different / so _____ .
   (clause 1)   (clause 2)

▶ 저희는 _____ .

▶ I like K-pop.

▶ I sang a lot of Korean songs / so _____.
    (clause 1)   (clause 2)

What do you wish you could have done but couldn't?

 → **?** →

▶ I wanted to go to a concert / but _____ / so 표를 **사지 못했어요.**
    (clause 1)   (clause 2)   (clause 3)

▶ I wanted to _____ / but _____ / so I couldn't _____.
    (clause 1)   (clause 2)   (clause 3)

Two pieces of advice that you want to give to 스티브 about Korean culture

▶ 한국에서는 집에서 신발을 안 **신으니까** /
                         (clause 1)

do not wear shoes inside the house.
                (clause 2)

▶ In the classroom,

don't _____.

Step 2. [Sharing] **You and your partner have different information to be included in a postcard. Exchange the information presented about your life during study abroad, what you wish you could have done, and advice for 스티브.**

notes

Step 3. [Writing] **Write a postcard to 스티브.**

☞ Use the worksheet on page 257 to complete the task.

Student B

Step 1. [Planning] Look at the information below. Come up with the missing information and think about how you are going to say the items in Korean. Try to use the new grammar features of Chapter 6. (You may change the order of the provided information and Korean expressions if needed.)

My life in Seoul

[cause]   [effect]

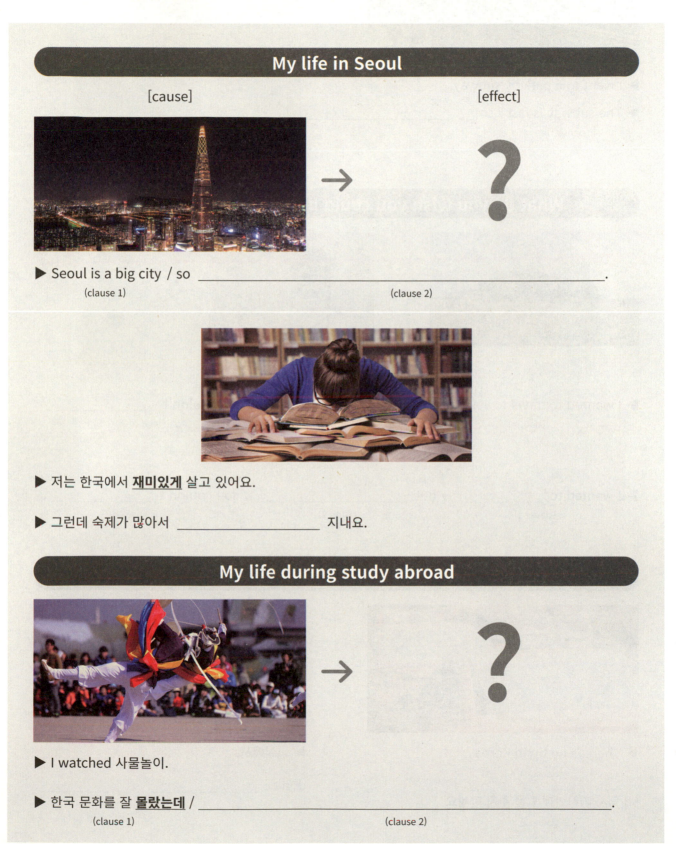

▶ Seoul is a big city / so _____.
   (clause 1)   (clause 2)

▶ 저는 한국에서 **재미있게** 살고 있어요.

▶ 그런데 숙제가 많아서 _____ 지내요.

My life during study abroad

[effect]

▶ I watched 사물놀이.

▶ 한국 문화를 잘 **몰랐는데** / _____.
   (clause 1)   (clause 2)

 →

▶ I went to a park by subway.

▶ The subway is fast / so _____.
   (clause 1)   (clause 2)

What do you wish you could have done but couldn't?

 → →

▶ I wanted to travel to Jeju Island / but _____ / so I couldn't _____.
   (clause 1)   (clause 2)   (clause 3)

▶ I wanted to _____ / but _____ / so I couldn't _____.
   (clause 1)   (clause 2)   (clause 3)

Two pieces of advice that you want to give to 스티브 about Korean culture

▶ There is no tip in Korea /
   (clause 1)

so 택시 기사한테 팁을 **주지 마세요**.
   (clause 2)

▶ 교실에서,

don't _____.

Step 2. [Sharing] **You and your partner have different information to be included in a postcard. Exchange the information presented about your life during study abroad, what you wish you could have done, and advice for 스티브.**

notes

Step 3. [Writing] **Write a postcard to 스티브.**

☞ Use the worksheet on page 257 to complete the task.

Chapter 06
Task 2

Write a Postcard to a Friend You Met during Study Abroad in Korea
Individual Writing

 Task Scenario

You are writing a postcard to 광수, a friend whom you met when you studied abroad in Korea. 광수 is going to travel to the U.S. and plans to come to see you at your university this summer. You are writing a postcard to 광수 to share what you have been doing lately, what you wanted to do in Korea but couldn't, what you want to do in the U.S. with 광수, and traveling advice for 광수.

Grammar in Action

1. Causal expression Noun(이)라서
2. Negative expression –지 못하다
3. Negative command –지 말다
4. Adverbial suffix –게
5. 르 irregular
6. Clausal connective –(으)니까

Helpful Words & Expressions

가수 singer	차 car	늦다 to be late
기말고사 final exam	케이팝 스타 K-pop star	(하고) 다르다 to be different
기말고사 기간 final exam week	택시 요금 taxi fare	따뜻하다 to be warm
꽃 flower	한국 문화 축제 Korean culture	만나다 to meet
노래 song	festival	머리를 자르다 to get a
노래방 noraebang	혼자 alone	haircut
머리 head, hair	걷다 to walk	모르다 to not know
미국 U.S.	길다 to be long	보다 to see
밤 night	길을 모르다 to not know	비싸다 to be expensive
방송국 TV station	how to get somewhere	아름답다 to be beautiful
봄 spring	길이 막히다 to be in a	위험하다 to be dangerous
수족관 aquarium	traffic jam	짧다 to be short
요즘 recently	꽃이 피다 to bloom	타다 to ride, get on
우버 Uber	노래를 부르다 to sing	

Step 1. [Planning] Look at the information below. Come up with the missing information and think about how you are going to say the items in Korean. Try to use the new grammar features of Chapter 6. (You may change the order of the provided information and Korean expressions if needed.)

My life in the U.S.

[cause]   [effect]

▶ 미국은 요즘 **봄이라서** / _____ .
  (clause 1)   (clause 2)

▶ Because it is Korean Cultural Festival Week / _____ .
  (clause 1)   (clause 2)

▶ 머리를 **잘라서** / _____ .
  (clause 1)   (clause 2)

▶ Because it is finals week / _____ .
  (clause 1)   (clause 2)

What were the things that you wanted to do but couldn't?

▶ I wanted to meet a K-pop star at a TV station / but _____ / so _____.
　　　　　　　(clause 1)　　　　　　　　　　　　　　　　　　　　(clause 2)　　　　　　　　　　　(clause 3)

▶ I wanted to go to 노래방 / but I didn't know many Korean songs / so _____.
　　　　(clause 1)　　　　　　　　　　　　　(clause 2)　　　　　　　　　　　　　(clause 3)

What do you want to do with 광수 in the U.S.?

[Suggestion 1]

[Reason: different from a Korean aquarium]

[Aquarium (수족관)]

▶ Because it is different from a Korean aquarium / _____.
　　　　　　　　　　(clause 1)　　　　　　　　　　　　　　　　　　　　(clause 2)

[Suggestion 2]

?　　　　　　　　　　[Reason: _____]

▶ _____ / _____.
　　　　　　(clause 1)　　　　　　　　　　　　　　　　(clause 2)

Four pieces of advice (with reasons) that you want to give to 광수 about traveling in the U.S.

[Advice 1]

[Reasons: traffic jam, expensive taxi fare]

▶ _____ / 택시를 **타지 말고** / 우버를 타세요.
　　　　(clause 1)　　　　　　　　　　　(clause 2)　　　(clause 3)

[Advice 2]

[Reasons: late night, dangerous]

▶ 늦은 밤에는 **위험하니까** / do not walk alone at night / but _____.
　　(clause 1)　　　　　　　　(clause 2)　　　　　　　　　(clause 3)

[Advice 3]

▶ _____ / _____.
　　　　(clause 1)　　　　　　　　　　　(clause 2)

[Advice 4]

▶ _____ / _____.
　　　　(clause 1)　　　　　　　　　　　(clause 2)

Step 2. [Writing] **Write a postcard to 광수.**

☞ Use the worksheet on page 261 to complete the task.

Send a Video Message to a Friend You Met during Study Abroad in Korea
Individual Speaking

✅ Task Scenario

You met 광수 while studying in Korea. 광수 is going to travel to the U.S. and plans to come to see you this summer. You want to send a video message to 광수 to share what you have been doing lately, what you wanted to do in Korea but couldn't, what you want to do in the U.S. with 광수, and traveling advice for 광수.

Grammar in Action

1. Causal expression Noun(이)라서
2. Negative expression –지 못하다
3. Negative command –지 말다
4. Adverbial suffix –게
5. 르 irregular
6. Clausal connective –(으)니까

Helpful Words & Expressions

가수 singer
기말고사 final exam
기말고사 기간 final exam week
꽃 flower
노래 song
노래방 noraebang
머리 head, hair
미국 U.S.
밤 night
방송국 TV station
봄 spring
수족관 aquarium
요즘 recently
우버 Uber

차 car
케이팝 스타 K-pop star
택시 요금 taxi fare
한국 문화 축제 Korean culture
    festival
혼자 alone
걷다 to walk
길다 to be long
길을 모르다 to not know
    how to get somewhere
길이 막히다 to be in a
    traffic jam
꽃이 피다 to bloom
노래를 부르다 to sing

늦다 to be late
(하고) 다르다 to be different
따뜻하다 to be warm
만나다 to meet
머리를 자르다 to get a
    haircut
모르다 to not know
보다 to see
비싸다 to be expensive
아름답다 to be beautiful
위험하다 to be dangerous
짧다 to be short
타다 to ride, get on

Step 1. **[Planning]** Look at the information below. Come up with the missing information and think about how you are going to say the items in Korean. Try to use the new grammar features of Chapter 6. (You may change the order of the provided information and Korean expressions if needed.)

My life in the U.S.

[cause] → [effect]

▶ 미국은 요즘 **봄이라서** / _____ .
　　(clause 1)　　　　　　　　　　　　　　　　(clause 2)

▶ Because it is Korean Cultural Festival Week / _____ .
　　　　　　(clause 1)　　　　　　　　　　　　　　　(clause 2)

▶ 머리를 **잘라서** / _____ .
　(clause 1)　　　　　　　　　　　　　(clause 2)

▶ Because it is finals week / _____ .
　　　　(clause 1)　　　　　　　　　　　　　(clause 2)

What were the things that you wanted to do but couldn't?

▶ I wanted to meet a K-pop star at a TV station / but _____ / so _____.
   (clause 1)   (clause 2)   (clause 3)

▶ I wanted to go to 노래방 / but I didn't know many Korean songs / so _____.
   (clause 1)   (clause 2)   (clause 3)

What do you want to do with 광수 in the U.S.?

[Suggestion 1]

[Reason: different from a Korean aquarium]

[Aquarium (수족관)]

▶ Because it is different from a Korean aquarium / _____.
   (clause 1)   (clause 2)

[Suggestion 2]

[Reason: _____]

▶ _____ / _____.
   (clause 1)   (clause 2)

Four pieces of advice (with reasons) that you want to give to 광수 about traveling in the U.S.

[Advice 1]

[Reasons: traffic jam, expensive taxi fare]

▶ _____ / 택시를 **타지 말고** / 우버를 타세요.
　　　(clause 1)　　　　　　　　　　　　(clause 2)　　　　(clause 3)

[Advice 2]

[Reasons: late night, dangerous]

▶ 늦은 밤에는 **위험하니까** / do not walk alone at night / but _____.
　　(clause 1)　　　　　　　　　(clause 2)　　　　　　　　　(clause 3)

[Advice 3]

▶ _____ / _____.
　　　(clause 1)　　　　　　　　　　　(clause 2)

[Advice 4]

▶ _____ / _____.
　　　(clause 1)　　　　　　　　　　　(clause 2)

Step 2. [Rehearsing] Rehearse a video message using the information presented. You can take notes to organize your video message.

Helpful information to elicit the content of your video message

1. Greetings
2. Description of your life in the U.S.
3. Four things that you couldn't do while studying abroad in Korea
4. Four things that you want to do with 광수 in the U.S.
5. Four pieces of advice including at least two reasons
6. Closing

notes

Send a Postcard to Your Friend

Step 3. [Recording] **Record your video message using your notes above.**

☞ Use the worksheet on page 265 to complete the task.

Task Scenario

You are going to send a postcard to your friend to tell them about the most memorable place that you have ever visited. Choose one of the most memorable places that you have visited and bring a postcard to write your message.

Materials to Bring

▶ A postcard

Grammar in Action

1. Causal expression Noun(이)라서
2. Negative expression –지 못하다
3. Negative command –지 말다
4. Adverbial suffix –게
5. 르 irregular
6. Clausal connective –(으)니까

Step 1. [Planning] Recall the tasks in this chapter and plan your postcard. Don't forget to bring in materials in advance before performing the task. Think about how to organize your postcard and choose a friend who will receive it. Try to use the new grammar features of Chapter 6 when you plan your message.

Helpful questions to elicit the content of your postcard

▶ How was the weather in the place that you visited?

▶ What were the activities that you enjoyed the most?

▶ What were the things that you couldn't do while visiting this place?

▶ What advice would you give to your friend if your friend visits this place?

notes

Step 2. [Writing] Write a message on the postcard to your friend using the information you planned.

☞ Use the worksheet on page 267 to complete the task.

Shopping Blog

CHAPTER

07

Blogs

Tasks

 Task 1
Write a Shopping Blog Post

 Task 2
Write a Blog Post for a Moving Sale

 Task 3
Create a Product Review Video on Your Shopping Blog

 Task 4
Real World Task: Create a Product Review Video on Your Shopping Blog

Chapter Learning Outcomes

Students will be able to:

1. Write a blog post about their experiences shopping or selling items

2. Use appropriate grammar forms to complete the following functions:
   (1) Provide information on what they can or cannot do with a certain item
   (2) Describe multiple actions that take place at the same time
   (3) Describe actions that take place in chronological order
   (4) Describe objects that are involved in an upcoming event

Grammar Focus

▶ **Expressing ability/inability –(으)ㄹ 수 있다/없다**

☞ Sentence ender –(으)ㄹ 수 있다/없다 indicates the possibility of a situation or a subject's ability/inability to do something.
e.g., 술을 마셔서 운전을 **할 수 없어요.**

▶ **Clausal connective –(으)면서**

☞ Clausal connective –(으)면서 expresses that two actions are being performed by the same subject at the same time.
e.g., 민수는 음악을 **들으면서** 한국어를 공부했어요.

▶ **Clausal connective –고 나서**

☞ Clausal connective –고 나서 indicates that the action in the first clause takes place before the action in the second clause.
e.g., 숙제를 **하고 나서** 청소했어요.

▶ **Noun-modifying form for adjective/verb (future) –(으)ㄹ**

☞ The noun-modifying form –(으)ㄹ is used with a verb or an adjective to modify a noun and indicates that the action or situation is going to happen.
e.g., 김민주 선생님께서는 내년에 저희한테 한국어를 **가르치실** 분이세요.

Write a Shopping Blog Post

Collaborative Speaking & Writing

Task Scenario

You and your partner went shopping at a department store. After shopping, you and your partner are writing a shopping blog post about how to go to the department store and about the items you and your partner bought.

Grammar in Action

1. Expressing ability/inability –(으)ㄹ 수 있다/없다
2. Clausal connective –(으)면서
3. Clausal Connective –고 나서
4. Noun-modifying form for adjective/verb (future) –(으)ㄹ

Helpful Words & Expressions

결혼식 wedding ceremony
고프로 GoPro
동안 during, for
면접 job interview
물건 thing, item
양복 suit
에스컬레이터 escalator
자전거 bicycle
졸업식 graduation ceremony
지하철 subway
카메라 camera
갖고 가다 to take
갖고 다니다 to carry around

갖고 오다 to bring
걸어가다 to go on foot
걸어다니다 to walk around
고르다 to choose
구경하다 to sightsee
까맣다 to be black
내려오다 to go down
드라이클리닝을 하다
    to get something dry cleaned
사다 to buy
사진을 찍다 to take a picture
쇼핑하다 to go shopping

신기하다 to be miraculous
쓰다 to use, write, wear
    (a hat, glasses)
여행하다 to travel
올라가다 to go up
입고 가다 to wear and go
입다 to wear
청소하다 to clean
충전하다 to charge
타고 가다 to go riding
타고 다니다 to ride around
타다 to ride, get on

Student A

Step 1. [Planning] Look at the information below. Come up with the missing information and think about how you are going to say the items in Korean. Try to use the new grammar features of Chapter 7. (You may change the order of the provided information and Korean expressions if needed.)

Your shopping trip

What you did while shopping

▶ While walking around / _____을/를 구경했어요.
   (clause 1)   (clause 2)

▶ _____ / I shopped.
              (clause 1)   (clause 2)

What you did after shopping

→ **?** →

_____

▶ 3시간 동안 **쇼핑하고 나서** / _____ .
   (clause 1)   (clause 2)

▶ _____ / 집에 갔어요.
              (clause 1)   (clause 2)

산 물건 ①: 까만 양복

What you bought

졸업식에서 **입을** 까만 양복

Things that you can do using the item

[job interview]   [wedding ceremony]

_____ 하고 _____ 에 **입고 갈 수 있어요.**

What you need to remember about the item

   →

After wearing the suit / you have to _____.
   (clause 1)   (clause 2)

산 물건 ②: _____

What you bought

I bought _____ that I will _____.

Things that you can do using the item

I can _____.

What you need to remember about the item

After _____ / you have to _____.
    (clause 1)   (clause 2)

Step 2. [Sharing] You and your partner have different information to be included in a blog post. Exchange the information presented about your shopping experience and the items that you bought.

notes

_____
_____
_____
_____

Step 3. [Writing] Write a blog post about your shopping experience and the items that you and your partner bought.

☞ Use the worksheet on page 271 to complete the task.

Student B

Step 1. **[Planning]** Look at the information below. Come up with the missing information and think about how you are going to say the items in Korean. Try to use the new grammar features of Chapter 7. (You may change the order of the provided information and Korean expressions if needed.)

Your shopping trip

What you did while shopping

▶ 에스컬레이터를 **타고 가면서** / 친구하고 _____.
　　　　　(clause 1)　　　　　　　　　　　　　　　　　　(clause 2)

▶ _____ / 쇼핑했어요.
　　　　　(clause 1)　　　　　　　　(clause 2)

What you did after shopping

I took a look at things that I will buy. → **?** → I ate dinner.

▶ After taking a look at things that I will buy / _____.
　　　　　　　　　　(clause 1)　　　　　　　　　　　　　　　　　(clause 2)

▶ _____ / I ate dinner.
　　　　　(clause 1)　　　　　　　　(clause 2)

산 물건 ① : 고프로

What you bought

while traveling in Korea

갖고 다닐 고프로

Things that you can do using the item

While riding a bicycle / I can take pictures.

(clause 1)　　　　　　　　(clause 2)

What you need to remember about the item

 →

After using the camera　　　/　　　you have to _____.

(clause 1)　　　　　　　　　　　　　　　(clause 2)

산 물건 ②: _____

What you bought

I bought _____ that I will _____.

Things that you can do using the item

I can _____.

What you need to remember about the item

After _____ / you have to _____.
       (clause 1)   (clause 2)

Step 2. [Sharing] You and your partner have different information to be included in the blog post. Exchange the information presented about your shopping experience and the items that you bought.

notes

- -

- -

- -

Step 3. [Writing] Write a blog post about your shopping experience and the items that you and your partner bought.

☞ Use the worksheet on page 271 to complete the task.

✓ Task Scenario

You are getting ready to move out of your current apartment, so you want to sell some of your belongings. You are writing a blog post for a moving sale. In your post, you will include information about one of the items, your contact information, and a few precautions to remember.

Grammar in Action

1. Expressing ability/inability –(으)ㄹ 수 있다/없다
2. Clausal connective –(으)면서
3. Clausal connective –고 나서
4. Noun-modifying form for adjective/verb (future) –(으)ㄹ

Helpful Words & Expressions

가격 price	이메일 email	들어가다 to enter
건물 building	이유 reason	들어오다 to come in
계단 stairs	전화번호 phone number	만들다 to make
공짜 free	정문 main gate	바쁘다 to be busy
공짜로 for free	지하철 역 subway station	보내다 to send
기숙사 dormitory	쯤 about	보다 to see
대학교 university	출구 exit	사다 to buy
문자 메시지 text message	커피 머신 coffee machine	쓰다 to use, write, wear
버스 정류장 bus stop	갖고 가다 to take	(a hat, glasses)
분 minute	갖다 드리다 to bring/take	올라오다 to come up
시청 city hall	something to	이사하다 to move (house)
아침 morning	someone	졸업하다 to graduate
여기 here	걷다 to walk	타다 to ride, get on
역 station	깨지다 to break	팔다 to sell
원래 가격 original price	내리다 to get off	할인하다 to give a discount

팔 물건: 커피 머신

Why you are selling the item

대학교를 **졸업하고 나서** / _____ .

(clause 1)   (clause 2)

Information about the coffee machine

커피 머신을 **살** 사람은 여기 보세요!

Good things	▶ 바쁜 아침에 커피를 빨리 **만들 수 있어요.** ▶ 커피를 **만들면서** / you can _____ . (clause 1) (clause 2)
Things that you need to remember	▶ After using the machine, / you have to _____ . (clause 1) (clause 2)
Price	▶ The original price: $250 ▶ The discounted price: $ _____ ▶ Reason for discount: _____ .

Further information

▶ A free item that you can give away: _____ .

▶ It can break / so I cannot send the coffee maker.
   (clause 1)   (clause 2)

▶ Please come to my dormitory / and 갖고 가세요.
   (clause 1)   (clause 2)

How to get to your dormitory

① Get off at Jackson (잭슨) Station.

→ ② Come out Exit 2 and 🚶 Walk for about _____ minutes.

→ ③ Transfer to Bus #15 at "시청 버스 정류장"

🚌 # _____ : Get on the # _____ bus

→ ④ Get off at the main gate of the university.

→ ⑤ 🚶 Walk across the university campus for about _____ minutes.

until you get to the _____ building.

→ ⑥ 🚶 Come up the stairs.

Step 2. [Writing] **Write your blog post for the moving sale.**

☞ Use the worksheet on page 275 to complete the task.

Chapter 07
Task 3

Create a Product Review Video on Your Shopping Blog
Individual Speaking

 Task Scenario

You are creating a product review video on your shopping blog for two products that you recently bought. In your post, you will describe what you bought, how you used the products, how they performed, and the pros and cons of the products, with reasons.

Grammar in Action

1. Expressing ability/inability –(으)ㄹ 수 있다/없다
2. Clausal connective –(으)면서
3. Clausal connective –고 나서
4. Noun-modifying form for adjective/verb (future) –(으)ㄹ

Helpful Words & Expressions

가격 price
고프로 GoPro
공짜 free
공짜로 for free
과자 cookie, snack
미니오븐 mini-oven
빨리 fast
빵 bread
요리 기구 cooking utensils
지난 주 last week
캐릭터 character
쿠키 cookies

파티 party
갖다드리다 to bring/take something to someone
갖고 가다 to take
만들다 to make
빠르다 to be fast
쉽다 to be easy
쓰다 to use, write, wear (a hat, glasses)
요리하다 to cook
작다 to be small

(을/를) 준비하다 to prepare
편리하다 to be convenient, comfortable
(이/가) 필요하다 to need
할인하다 to give a discount

Product information ①: 미니오븐

★★★★☆

When / where you bought the item

▶ Last week

▶ At _____

Why you bought the item

▶ 파티 음식을 **만들** 미니오븐이 필요해요.

▶ I needed an oven that I will _____.

What you can do using the item & some advantages

▶ Convenient

▶ 음식을 쉽고 빠르게 **요리할 수 있어요**.

▶ 다른 일을 **하면서** / I can _____.

     (clause 1)   (clause 2)

Things that you need to remember & some disadvantages

▶ 이 미니오븐을 **쓰고 나서** / _____.

     (clause 1)   (clause 2)

▶ It's too small / so you cannot _____.

     (clause 1)   (clause 2)

A person who will enjoy the item

▶ It will be good for a person who _____.

Product information ② : 고프로

When / where you bought the item

▶ Last weekend

▶ At _____

Why you bought the item

▶ I bought the GoPro that I will carry around while traveling.

▶ I needed the GoPro that I will _____ every day.

What you can do using the item & some advantages

▶ I can take pictures while riding a bicycle.

▶ I can _____ / while _____ .
                   (clause 1)   (clause 2)

Things that you need to remember & some disadvantages

▶ A little expensive

▶ You cannot _____ .

▶ After using this camera / you have to charge it once a day.
      (clause 1)   (clause 2)

A person who will enjoy the item

▶ 이 고프로는 _____ 사람한테 좋을 거예요.

Step 2. [Rehearsing] Rehearse your product review video using the information presented. You can take notes to organize your video.

Helpful information to elicit the content of your video

1. Greetings
2. Personal introduction
3. Description of the items
   · When and where you bought the items
   · Why you bought the items
4. What you can do with the items
5. Things that people need to remember when using the items
6. To whom you will recommend the items
7. Closing

notes

Step 3. [Recording] Record your product review video using your notes you planned.

☞ Use the worksheet on page 279 to complete the task.

Chapter 07
Task 4:
Real World Task

Create a Product Review Video on Your Shopping Blog
Individual Speaking

 Task Scenario

You are going to create a product review video about one of the products that you bought. Think about which item you will describe, and include how to use it, the pros and cons of the product, and things to remember when using the item.

Materials to Bring

▶ An actual product that you will introduce (If you cannot bring one, you can bring a photo instead.)
▶ An electronic device for making your product review video (e.g., laptop, tablet, smartphone)

Grammar in Action

1. Expressing ability/inability –(으)ㄹ 수 있다/없다
2. Clausal connective –(으)면서
3. Clausal connective –고 나서
4. Noun-modifying form for adjective/verb (future) –(으)ㄹ

Step 1. [Planning] Recall the tasks in this chapter and plan your product review video. Don't forget to bring in materials in advance before performing the task. Think about how you are going to organize your product review video. Try to use the new grammar features of Chapter 7 when you plan your product review video.

Helpful questions to elicit the content of your product review

▶ What did you buy?

▶ When and why did you buy the item?

▶ How were you able to use the item, and how did it perform?

▶ What do you have to do after using the item?

▶ What are the pros and cons of the item?

▶ To whom would you recommend the item?

Step 2. [Rehearsing] Rehearse your product review video using the information you planned. You can take notes to organize your video.

notes

Step 3. [Recording] Make your product review video using the information you prepared.

☞ Use the worksheet on page 281 to complete the task.

CHAPTER

08

Vlogs

Tasks

 Task 1
Make a Vlog Entry Comparing Korean Restaurants before Visiting

Task 2
Make a Vlog Entry after Visiting a Korean Restaurant

Task 3
Write a Vlog Entry Script about Visiting Korea

Task 4
Create a Vlog Entry about Your Favorite Places in Town

Chapter Learning Outcomes

Students will be able to:
1. Make a Vlog to share their personal experiences

2. Use appropriate grammar forms to complete the following functions:
   (1) Express what they tried to do
   (2) Provide a reason or describe the cause of an action in a formal manner
   (3) Indicate the beneficiary of an action while showing respect to the beneficiary
   (4) Express negative meaning in a formal manner

▶ Auxiliary verb –어/아 보다

☞ **Auxiliary verb –어/아 보다 is used to indicate the subject's experience or attempt at doing something.**
e.g., 지난 주말에 처음으로 불고기를 **먹어 봤어요.**

▶ Nominalization –기

☞ **If a verb stem is attached to the nominalizer –기, the verb behaves like other nouns.**
e.g., 제 취미는 영화 **보기**, 음악 **듣기**, **요리하기예요.**

▶ Causal expression –기 때문에

☞ **When a clausal predicate (i.e., verb or adjective) is nominalized with –기, it can be attached with 때문에 and indicates that the clause is the reason for or cause of the main clause.**
e.g., 제 친구는 고등학교 때 케이팝을 **좋아했기 때문에** 지금도 한국 노래를 잘해요.

▶ Benefactive (humble) –어/아 드리다

☞ **The auxiliary verb -어/아 드리다 is a humble expression of –어/아 주다 which expresses that the subject does something for the benefit of someone else. -어/아 드리다 is used when the subject needs to show respect to the beneficiary due to seniority or higher social status.**
e.g., 저는 이번 크리스마스 때 할머니께 예쁜 장갑을 **사 드렸어요.**

▶ Negative expression –지 않다

☞ **If negative expression form –지 않다 is used with a verb or adjective, it implies a negative meaning such as "does not" or "is not." It is a little bit more formal than the short form negation "안" and more frequently used in writing.**
e.g., 이번 학기에는 전공 수업을 들어야 돼서 한국어 수업을 **듣지 않았어요.**

Chapter 08
Task 1

Make a Vlog Entry Comparing Korean Restaurants before Visiting
Collaborative Speaking

Task Scenario

You and your partner are going to post a vlog entry about two Korean restaurants that you both want to try before visiting one. In your video, introduce two restaurants that you have heard about from friends/on-line reviews in terms of their location, menu, pros and cons of each restaurant, and what you want to try at each restaurant. Then, decide which restaurant you want to visit with your partner.

Grammar in Action

1. Auxiliary verb –어/아 보다
2. Nominalization –기
3. Causal expression –기 때문에
4. Benefactive (humble) –어/아 드리다
5. Negative expression –지 않다

Helpful Words & Expressions

갈비 galbi	중식당 chinese restaurant	불편하다 to be inconvenient
냉면 naengmyeon	테이블 table	비싸다 to be expensive
면 noodle	한식당 korean restaurant	자르다 to cut
영어 english	가깝다 to be close, near	(을/를) 잘하다 to be good at
의자 chair	길다 to be long	주문하다 to order (food)
짜장면 jjajangmyeon	넓다 to be spacious	주차하다 to park
짬뽕 jjamppong	달다 to be sweet	차다 to be cold
젓가락 chopsticks	맛있다 to be delicious	크다 to be big
젓가락질 use of chopsticks	맵다 to be spicy	편하다 to be convenient
종업원 employer, server	멀다 to be far	
주차장 parking lot	배우다 to learn	

Student A

Step 1. [Planning] Look at the information below. Come up with the missing information and think about how you are going to say the items in Korean. Try to use the new grammar features of Chapter 8. (You may change the order of the provided information and Korean expressions if needed.)

Restaurant and location

*These pictures are given to help you generate ideas. You may use these pictures to narrate a story.

[한식당]

▶ 한식당은 **멀기 때문에** / _____.
      (clause 1)   (clause 2)

Description of popular menu items at the restaurant

▶ 냉면

  • It is very cold.

  • 면이 길어서 종업원이 면을 **잘라 드려요**. So, it is easy to eat.

▶ 갈비

  • It is not too sweet.

  • _____ / _____.
      (clause 1)   (clause 2)

Pros and cons

▶ It is nice because the food is delicious and not too expensive.

▶ It is difficult to park because the parking lot is not spacious.

What you want to try at the restaurant

▶ 젓가락질 **배우기**

▶ _____.

▶ _____.

Step 2. [Sharing/Rehearsing] You and your partner have different information to be included in a vlog entry. Exchange the information presented about two restaurants, discuss their popular menu items and pros and cons, and decide what you would want to try at the restaurants. Then, discuss and decide which restaurant you and your partner want to try for the next vlog entry. After sharing the information, rehearse the vlog collaboratively with your partner before recording.

▶ 같이 갈 식당: _____

▶ Reason: _____ **기 때문에 가 보고** 싶어요.

notes

Step 3. [Recording] Record your vlog entry.

☞ Use the worksheet on page 283 to complete the task.

Student B

Step 1. [Planning] Look at the information below. Come up with the missing information and think about how you are going to say the items in Korean. Try to use the new grammar features of Chapter 8. (You may change the order of the provided information and Korean expressions if needed.)

Restaurant and location

*These pictures are given to help you generate ideas. You may use these pictures to narrate a story.

[중식당]

▶ The Chinese restaurant is close so / _____ .

      (clause 1)   (clause 2)

Description of popular menu items at the restaurant

▶ 짜장면

  • It is sweet.

  • It is not spicy so 매운 음식을 못 먹는 사람도 **먹기** 좋아요.

▶ 짬뽕

  • It is very spicy.

  • _____ / _____ .

      (clause 1)   (clause 2)

Pros and cons

▶ 테이블이 크고 의자가 **불편하지 않아요**.

▶ The employees are not good at speaking English.

What you want to try at the restaurant

▶ 한국어로 **주문하기**

▶ _____ .

▶ _____ .

Step 2. [Sharing/Rehearsing] You and your partner have different information to be included in a vlog entry. Exchange the information presented about two restaurants, discuss their popular menu items and pros and cons, and decide what you would want to try at the restaurants Then, discuss and decide which restaurant you and your partner want to try for the next vlog entry. After sharing the information, rehearse the vlog collaboratively with your partner before recording.

▶ 같이 갈 식당: _____

▶ Reason: _____ **기 때문에 가 보고** 싶어요.

notes

Step 3. [Recording] Record your vlog entry.

☞ Use the worksheet on page 283 to complete the task.

Chapter 08
Task 2

Make a Vlog Entry after Visiting a Korean Restaurant
Individual Speaking

 Task Scenario

You are going to post a vlog entry about your experience at a Korean restaurant. Due to the fact that you and your partner have different schedules, you could not visit the restaurant together. Instead, you visited one of the restaurants with your family. In the vlog entry, share why you couldn't go to the restaurant with your partner, what you and your family did at the restaurant, how the food was, and the pros and cons of the restaurant.

Grammar in Action

1. Auxiliary verb –어/아 보다
2. Nominalization –기
3. Causal expression –기 때문에
4. Benefactive (humble) –어/아 드리다
5. Negative expression –지 않다

Helpful Words & Expressions

가위 scissors	자리 seat	맵다 to be spicy
갈비 galbi	젓가락 chopsticks	멀다 to be far
냉면 naengmyeon	종업원 employee, server	시키다 to order
다음 번 next time	주말 weekend	예약하다 to book, reserve
맛 taste	중식당 chinese restaurant	유명하다 to be famous
면 noodle	처음으로 for the first time	자르다 to cut
미리 in advance	특징 characteristic	주문하다 to order (food)
순두부찌개 soft tofu stew	파트너 partner	차갑다 to be cold
식당 restaurant	한식당 korean restaurant	추천하다 to recommend
아주 very	기다리다 to wait	
여러분 everyone	길다 to be long	

[Planning] **Look at the information below. Come up with the missing information and think about how you are going to say the items in Korean. Try to use the new grammar features of Chapter 8. (You may change the order of the provided information and Korean expressions if needed.)**

The reason why you couldn't go with your partner

▶ My partner _____ last Sunday / so we couldn't _____.
　　　　　　　　　　(clause 1)　　　　　　　　　　　　　　　　　　　　　　　　(clause 2)

What the restaurant was like

▶ **주말이었기 때문에** _____.

▶ My family and I waited about _____ minutes because we didn't reserve a table in advance.

What I ordered at the restaurant

▶ 주문한 음식: 갈비

▶ 특징(characteristics): 유명하다.

▶ 맛: 아주 맵다.
Because it was too spicy, I did not eat it all.

What my family ordered at the restaurant

My younger sister

▶ 주문한 음식: 순두부찌개

▶ 맛: **맵지 않다**. 맛있다.

▶ 제 여동생은 _____.

My mother & my grandmother

▶ 주문한 음식: 냉면

▶ 특징(characteristics): 면이 길다.

▶ 어머니하고 할머니는 처음으로 냉면을 **시켜 보셨는데** /

(clause 1)

I cut the noodles for them.

(clause 2)

▶ My grandmother didn't like it

because it wasn't _____.

Things I tried at 한식당

▶ 젓가락으로 한국 음식 **먹어 보기**

▶ _____.

Information about 중식당 that you and your partner want to try next time

▶ The Chinese restaurant is not far from the university, / so 학교에서 **가기** 좋아요.

(clause 1)   (clause 2)

▶ It is good to _____ at the restaurant because _____.

▶ I want to try to _____.

notes

Step 2. [Rehearsing] Rehearse a vlog entry about the restaurant you and your family visited using the information presented. You can take notes to organize your vlog entry.

Helpful information to elicit the content of your vlog entry

1. Greetings

2. The purpose of the vlog entry

3. The reason why you couldn't go with your partner

4. Information about the restaurant and the food

   · What the restaurant was like

   · The dishes that you and your family ordered

   · What the foods you and your family ordered were like

   · What you and your family did

5. Things that you tried

6. Information about 중식당 that you and your partner want to visit

7. Closing by recommending the restaurant to your viewers:

   "이렇게 저는 주말에 한식당에 가 봤는데요.

   _____ **기 때문에** 좋았어요. 여러분도 한번 **가 보세요.**"

notes

_____

_____

_____

_____

Step 3. [Recording] Record your vlog entry using the notes you planned.

☞ Use the worksheet on page 285 to complete the task.

Task Scenario

You are going to post a vlog entry about your plan for a trip to Korea. You are writing a script before making your vlog entry. In your script, include the places you are going to visit, what you are going to eat, and what you are going to do in Korea.

Grammar in Action

1. Auxiliary verb –어/아 보다
2. Nominalization –기
3. Causal expression –기 때문에
4. Benefactive (humble) –어/아 드리다
5. Negative expression –지 않다

Helpful Words & Expressions

게스트하우스 guesthouse
곳 place
냉면 naengmyeon
면 noodle
모래 축제 sand festival
문화 culture
밀면 milmyeon
바닷가 beach
부산 Busan
비빔밥 bibimbap
수영 swimming
순두부찌개 soft tofu stew
요리 수업 cooking class

이유 reason
장소 place
전주 Jeonju
집 house
특징 characteristics
한복 hanbok
한옥 마을 hanok village
해운대 Haeundae
경험하다 to experience
구경하다 to sightsee
길다 to be long
놀다 to play, hang out
(하고) 다르다 to be different

달다 to be sweet
수업을 듣다 to take a class
만들다 to make
맵다 to be spicy
배우다 to learn
비싸다 to be expensive
수영하다 to swim
유명하다 to be famous
입다 to wear (clothes)
좋아하다 to like
차다 to be cold

Look at the information below. Come up with the missing information and think about how you are going to say the items in Korean. Try to use the new grammar features of Chapter 8. (You may change the order of the provided information and Korean expressions if needed.)

Place to visit ①: 부산 (Busan)

*These pictures are given to help you generate ideas. You may use these pictures to narrate a story.

▶ **먹어 보고** 싶은 음식: 밀면 (Milmyeon)
• The reason why you want to try 밀면: 냉면하고 **다르기 때문에**

▶ Characteristics:
• 찬 음식
• 면이 길다.
• **맵지 않고** 달다.

▶ The place you want to go to: 해운대 바닷가

▶ The reason why you want to go to 해운대 바닷가: It is famous in Busan.

▶ Things you want to try:
1) 모래 축제에서 **놀기**
• Reason: I do not like swimming.

2) _____.

▶ The food you want to try: 비빔밥

• The reason why you want to try 비빔밥: _____ .

▶ Activities you want to try: taking a cooking class where I can learn how to make 비빔밥

▶ The place where you want to go: 한옥 마을 (hanok village)

▶ Things you want to try:

1) Sleeping in 한옥 게스트하우스

• Reason: It is not too expensive and I want to experience Korean house culture.

2) Sightseeing at 한옥 마을 wearing 한복

3) _____ .

Step 2. [Writing] **Write your vlog entry script using the information.**

☞ Use the worksheet on page 287 to complete the task.

Chapter 08
Task 4:
Real World Task

Create a Vlog Entry about Your Favorite Places in Town
Individual Speaking

✅ Task Scenario

You are creating a vlog entry about your favorite places in town. Introduce places, foods, and activities with detailed information. Then, suggest to the audience why they should visit your neighborhood, and provide information about why you recommend the places, foods, and activities that you suggest.

Materials to Bring

▶ Some pictures of your favorite places in town
▶ An electronic device for making your vlog entry (e.g., laptop, smartphone, tablet)

Grammar in Action

1. Auxiliary verb –어/아 보다
2. Nominalization –기
3. Causal expression –기 때문에
4. Benefactive (humble) –어/아 드리다
5. Negative expression –지 않다

Step 1. [Planning] Recall the tasks in this chapter and plan your vlog entry. Make sure to bring in materials in advance before performing the task. Think about how you are going to organize your vlog entry. Try to use the new grammar features of Chapter 8 when you plan your script.

Helpful questions to elicit the content of your vlog entry

▶ Which places, foods, and activities are popular in your favorite places in town?

▶ Which places would you suggest to the audience? Provide reasons why.

▶ Which foods would you suggest to the audience? Provide reasons why.

▶ Which activities would you suggest to the audience? Provide reasons why.

▶ Any additional information on things to enjoy while visiting your neighborhood? What are they?

Step 2. [Rehearsing] Rehearse the vlog entry you planned. You can take notes to organize the content.

notes
_____
_____
_____
_____
_____
_____

Step 3. [Recording] Make your vlog entry using the information you prepared.

☞ Use the worksheet on page 291 to complete the task.

Appendices

Vocabulary Index 1 (Korean-English)

가

Korean	English	Tasks (Ch -> Chapter)
가게	store	Ch04 Task 2
가격	price	Ch03 Task 1, Ch03 Task 2, Ch07 Task 1, Ch07 Task 3
가깝다	to be near	Ch03 Task 2, Ch08 Task 1
가다	to go	Ch04 Task 2, Ch04 Task 3
가르치다	to teach	Ch02 Task 3, Ch06 Task 1
가방	bag	Ch04 Task 2
가수	singer	Ch06 Task 2, Ch06 Task 3
가위	scissors	Ch08 Task 2
가을	fall, autumn	Ch02 Task 2
갈비	galbi	Ch03 Task 1, Ch03 Task 2, Ch08 Task 1, Ch08 Task 2
감기	cold (noun)	Ch05 Task 2, Ch05 Task 3
감기에 걸리다	to catch a cold	Ch05 Task 2, Ch05 Task 3
갖고 가다	to take	Ch07 Task 1, Ch07 Task 2, Ch07 Task 3
갖고 다니다	to carry around	Ch07 Task 1
갖고 오다	to bring	Ch07 Task 1
갖다 드리다	to bring/take something to someone	Ch07 Task 2, Ch07 Task 3
개	counting unit	Ch03 Task 3
거리	distance	Ch03 Task 2, Ch03 Task 3
건물	building	Ch07 Task 2
걷다	to walk	Ch06 Task 2, Ch06 Task 3, Ch07 Task 2
걸리다	to take (time)	Ch03 Task 1
걸어가다	to go on foot	Ch07 Task 1
걸어다니다	to walk around	Ch07 Task 1
게스트하우스	guesthouse	Ch08 Task 3
결혼 축하 파티	reception	Ch05 Task 2, Ch05 Task 3
결혼식	wedding ceremony	Ch05 Task 2, Ch05 Task 3, Ch07 Task 1
결혼하다	to marry	Ch04 Task 2, Ch04 Task 3, Ch05 Task 2, Ch05 Task 3
경험하다	to experience	Ch08 Task 3
계단	stairs	Ch07 Task 2
계획	plan	Ch03 Task 2
고등학교	high school	Ch04 Task 2
고르다	to choose	Ch07 Task 1
고프로	GoPro	Ch07 Task 1, Ch07 Task 3'
골프	golf	Ch03 Task 1
골프를 치다	to play golf	Ch03 Task 1
곳	place	Ch04 Task 2, Ch08 Task 3
공원	park	Ch03 Task 1, Ch06 Task 1
공짜	free	Ch07 Task 2, Ch07 Task 3
공짜로	for free	Ch07 Task 2, Ch07 Task 3
과목	subject	Ch02 Task 1, Ch02 Task 2, Ch02 Task 3
과자	cookie, snack	Ch07 Task 3
굉장히	very much	Ch02 Task 1, Ch02 Task 2, Ch02 Task 3
교수님	professor	Ch01 Task 3, Ch02 Task 1, Ch02 Task 2, Ch02 Task 3, Ch05 Task 2, Ch05 Task 3
교실	classroom	Ch06 Task 1
교통	transportation	Ch02 Task 1, Ch02 Task 2, Ch02 Task 3
교환	exchange	Ch02 Task 2, Ch02 Task 3
교회에 가다	to go to church	Ch03 Task 1
구경하다	to sightsee	Ch07 Task 1, Ch08 Task 3
국제	international	Ch02 Task 2, Ch02 Task 3
귀걸이	earring	Ch04 Task 2, Ch04 Task 3
그때	at that time	Ch04 Task 2
그림	picture/drawing	Ch01 Task 3
글씨	handwriting	Ch05 Task 1
기간	period, term	Ch02 Task 2
기다리다	to wait	Ch08 Task 2
기말고사	final exam	Ch06 Task 2, Ch06 Task 3
기말고사 기간	final exam week	Ch06 Task 2, Ch06 Task 3
기숙사	dormitory	Ch02 Task 1, Ch03 Task 3, Ch07 Task 2
기숙사비	boarding expenses	Ch02 Task 2
길다	to be long	Ch01 Task 1, Ch01 Task 2, Ch01 Task 3, Ch06 Task 2, Ch06 Task 3, Ch08 Task 1, Ch08 Task 2, Ch08 Task 3
길을 모르다	to not know how to get somewhere	Ch06 Task 2, Ch06 Task 3
길이 막히다	to be blocked, congested	Ch02 Task 1, Ch02 Task 2, Ch02 Task 3
길이 막히다	to be in a traffic jam	Ch06 Task 2, Ch06 Task 3
김치	kimchi	Ch02 Task 3
까맣다	to be black	Ch04 Task 1, Ch04 Task 2, Ch04 Task 3, Ch07 Task 1
깨끗하다	to be clean	Ch02 Task 2
깨지다	to break	Ch07 Task 2
꽃	flower	Ch04 Task 1, Ch06 Task 2, Ch06 Task 3
꽃이 피다	to bloom	Ch06 Task 2, Ch06 Task 3
꾸미다	to decorate	Ch05 Task 1
끝나다	to end	Ch04 Task 2
끼다	to wear (gloves, a ring, glasses)	Ch04 Task 1, Ch04 Task 2, Ch04 Task 3

나

Korean	English	Tasks (Ch -> Chapter)
날씨	weather	Ch01 Task 2, Ch01 Task 3, Ch03 Task 1
남동생	younger brother	Ch03 Task 1
낫다	to recover	Ch05 Task 2, Ch05 Task 3
내려오다	to go down	Ch07 Task 1
내리다	to get off	Ch07 Task 2
냉면	naengmyeon	Ch08 Task 1, Ch08 Task 2, Ch08 Task 3
넓다	to be spacious	Ch08 Task 1
네타이	necktie	Ch04 Task 2, Ch04 Task 3
노랗다	to be yellow	Ch04 Task 1, Ch04 Task 2, Ch04 Task 3
노래	song	Ch06 Task 1, Ch06 Task 2, Ch06 Task 3
노래를 부르다	to sing a song	Ch06 Task 1, Ch06 Task 2, Ch06 Task 3
노래방	noraebang	Ch02 Task 3, Ch06 Task 2, Ch06 Task 3
노래하다	to sing a song	Ch02 Task 3
놀다	to play, hang out	Ch02 Task 1, Ch02 Task 2, Ch02 Task 3, Ch08 Task 3
눈이 오다	to snow	Ch03 Task 1, Ch03 Task 2, Ch04 Task 2
뉴욕	New York	Ch04 Task 2
늦게	late	Ch03 Task 2
늦다	to be late	Ch02 Task 1, Ch02 Task 2, Ch02 Task 3, Ch06 Task 2, Ch06 Task 3

다

Korean	English	Tasks (Ch -> Chapter)
(하고) 다르다	to be different	Ch06 Task 1, Ch06 Task 2, Ch06 Task 3, Ch08 Task 3
다 차다	to be full	Ch02 Task 1
다음 번	next time	Ch08 Task 2
다음 학기	next semester	Ch02 Task 1
단점	disadvantages	Ch02 Task 2, Ch02 Task 3
닫는 시간	closing time	Ch03 Task 3
달다	to be sweet	Ch08 Task 1, Ch08 Task 3
달러	dollar	Ch03 Task 1
닭갈비	chicken galbi	Ch03 Task 2
대학교	university	Ch06 Task 1, Ch07 Task 2

댁	house (honorific)	Ch01 Task 1, Ch01 Task 2, Ch05 Task 2, Ch05 Task 3
더블 데이트	double date	Ch03 Task 2
더블 데이트를 하다	to double-date	Ch03 Task 2
덥다	to be hot	Ch01 Task 3, Ch06 Task 1
도서관	library	Ch03 Task 3
도시	city	Ch04 Task 2, Ch06 Task 1
돈	money	Ch05 Task 1
돈이 들다	to cost	Ch03 Task 1
돕다	to help	Ch05 Task 2, Ch05 Task 3
동안	during, for	Ch05 Task 1, Ch07 Task 1
동창회	reunion	Ch04 Task 2, Ch04 Task 3
두 번째	second	Ch01 Task 2
드라마	drama	Ch02 Task 1
드라이클리닝을 하다	to get something dry cleaned	Ch07 Task 1
드리다	to give (humble)	Ch01 Task 1, Ch01 Task 2, Ch01 Task 3
드시다	to eat (honorific)	Ch01 Task 1, Ch01 Task 2, Ch01 Task 3
들어가다	to enter	Ch07 Task 2
들어오다	to come in	Ch07 Task 2
디즈니랜드	Disneyland	Ch04 Task 1
따뜻하다	to be warm	Ch01 Task 1, Ch06 Task 2, Ch06 Task 3
떡	rice cake	Ch01 Task 3, Ch02 Task 3
떡국	rice cake soup	Ch01 Task 1

라

랩	lab	Ch03 Task 3
로스 앤젤레스	Los Angeles	Ch04 Task 1
룸메이트	roommate	Ch02 Task 1, Ch02 Task 2, Ch02 Task 3, Ch05 Task 2, Ch05 Task 3, Ch06 Task 1
리조트	resort	Ch03 Task 1

마

마시다	to drink	Ch03 Task 3
만나다	to meet	Ch04 Task 1, Ch04 Task 2, Ch04 Task 3, Ch06 Task 2, Ch06 Task 3
만들다	to make	Ch02 Task 3, Ch03 Task 1, Ch04 Task 2, Ch04 Task 3, Ch07 Task 2, Ch07 Task 3, Ch08 Task 3
많다	to be many, much	Ch01 Task 1, Ch01 Task 3
맛	taste	Ch03 Task 2, Ch08 Task 2
맛없다	to taste bad	Ch01 Task 3
맛있다	to be delicious	Ch01 Task 3, Ch08 Task 1
매다	to wear (a necktie)	Ch04 Task 1, Ch04 Task 2, Ch04 Task 3
맵다	to be spicy	Ch02 Task 3, Ch03 Task 2, Ch08 Task 1, Ch08 Task 2, Ch08 Task 3
머리	head, hair	Ch05 Task 2, Ch05 Task 3, Ch06 Task 2, Ch06 Task 3
머리를 자르다	to get a haircut	Ch06 Task 2, Ch06 Task 3
멀다	to be far	Ch03 Task 2, Ch08 Task 1, Ch08 Task 2
멀리	far, far away	Ch02 Task 1
멋지다	to be nice	Ch01 Task 2, Ch01 Task 3
메뉴	menu	Ch02 Task 2, Ch02 Task 3
면	noodle	Ch08 Task 1, Ch08 Task 2, Ch08 Task 3
면담 시간	office hours	Ch05 Task 1
면접	job interview	Ch07 Task 1
모래 축제	sand festival	Ch08 Task 3
모래성	sandcastle	Ch04 Task 1
모르다	to not know	Ch06 Task 2, Ch06 Task 3
모자	cap, hat	Ch04 Task 2, Ch04 Task 3, Ch06 Task 1
모자를 쓰다	to wear a cap	Ch06 Task 1

목	neck, throat	Ch05 Task 2, Ch05 Task 3
목걸이	necklace	Ch04 Task 2, Ch04 Task 3
문을 닫다	to close	Ch03 Task 2, Ch03 Task 3
문을 열다	to open	Ch03 Task 2
문자 메시지	text message	Ch07 Task 2
문화	culture	Ch02 Task 1, Ch02 Task 2, Ch02 Task 3, Ch06 Task 1, Ch08 Task 3
물가	cost of living	Ch05 Task 1
물건	thing, item	Ch07 Task 1
미국	U.S.A	Ch06 Task 2, Ch06 Task 3
미니	Minnie Mouse	Ch04 Task 1
미니오븐	mini-oven	Ch07 Task 3
미리	in advance	Ch08 Task 2
미키	Mickey Mouse	Ch04 Task 1
밀면	milmyeon	Ch08 Task 3

바

바꾸다	to change	Ch05 Task 1
바닷가	beach	Ch03 Task 1, Ch04 Task 1, Ch08 Task 3
바람이 불다	to be windy	Ch03 Task 1
바쁘다	to be busy	Ch06 Task 1, Ch07 Task 2
바지	pants	Ch04 Task 2, Ch04 Task 3
밖	outside	Ch02 Task 1, Ch02 Task 2, Ch02 Task 3
반지	ring	Ch04 Task 1, Ch04 Task 2, Ch04 Task 3
발표	presentation	Ch05 Task 2, Ch05 Task 3
밤	night	Ch06 Task 2, Ch06 Task 3
방송국	TV station	Ch06 Task 2, Ch06 Task 3
배우다	to learn	Ch02 Task 1, Ch02 Task 3, Ch08 Task 1, Ch08 Task 3
백화점	department store	Ch04 Task 1
버스 정류장	bus stop	Ch07 Task 2
보내다	to send	Ch05 Task 1, Ch07 Task 2
보다	to see	Ch06 Task 2, Ch06 Task 3, Ch07 Task 2
보통	usually	Ch03 Task 1, Ch03 Task 2
복잡하다	to be crowded	Ch02 Task 1, Ch02 Task 2, Ch02 Task 3
봄	spring	Ch06 Task 2, Ch06 Task 3
봄방학	spring break	Ch03 Task 1
뵙다	to see (honorific)	Ch05 Task 1
부모님	parents	Ch05 Task 2, Ch05 Task 3
부산	Busan	Ch08 Task 3
부스	booth	Ch01 Task 3
분	minute	Ch07 Task 2
불고기	bulgogi	Ch03 Task 1
불편하다	to be inconvenient, uncomfortable	Ch02 Task 1, Ch02 Task 2, Ch02 Task 3, Ch08 Task 1
붙이다	to put (a poster) on	Ch05 Task 1
비가 오다	to rain	Ch03 Task 1
비빔밥	bibimbap	Ch02 Task 3, Ch08 Task 3
비싸다	to be expensive	Ch01 Task 1, Ch01 Task 2, Ch03 Task 2, Ch06 Task 2, Ch06 Task 3, Ch08 Task 3
비행기	airplane	Ch03 Task 1
비행기표	airline ticket	Ch03 Task 1
빌려주다	to lend	Ch05 Task 1
빌리다	to borrow	Ch05 Task 1
빠르다	to be fast	Ch06 Task 1, Ch07 Task 3
빨갛다	to be red	Ch04 Task 1, Ch04 Task 2, Ch04 Task 3
빨리	fast	Ch07 Task 3
빵	bread	Ch07 Task 3

사

사다	to buy	Ch04 Task 1, Ch04 Task 2, Ch04 Task 3, Ch06 Task 1, Ch07 Task 1, Ch07 Task 2

사람들	people	Ch01 Task 1
사람이 많다	to be crowded	Ch03 Task 1
사물놀이	samullori (traditional Korean instrumental music)	Ch06 Task 1
사진	picture	Ch05 Task 2, Ch05 Task 3
사진을 찍다	to take a picture	Ch01 Task 1, Ch01 Task 2, Ch01 Task 3, Ch03 Task 1, Ch04 Task 1, Ch05 Task 2, Ch05 Task 3, Ch07 Task 1
산타클로스	Santa Claus	Ch04 Task 2
살다	to live	Ch06 Task 1
삼겹살	pork belly	Ch03 Task 2
새벽	dawn	Ch03 Task 3
샌드위치	sandwich	Ch03 Task 3
생물학	biology	Ch03 Task 3
생신	birthday (honorific)	Ch01 Task 2
서울	Seoul	Ch06 Task 1
선글라스	sunglasses	Ch04 Task 1, Ch04 Task 3
선물	present, gift	Ch01 Task 1
성함	name (honorific)	Ch01 Task 1
센트럴파크	Central Park	Ch04 Task 2
셔츠	shirts	Ch04 Task 1, Ch04 Task 2, Ch04 Task 3
소개하다	to introduce	Ch01 Task 2, Ch05 Task 1
쇼핑하다	to go shopping	Ch04 Task 2, Ch07 Task 1
수업	class, lesson	Ch06 Task 1
수업에 늦다	to be late for class	Ch02 Task 1
수업을 듣다	to take a class	Ch02 Task 1, Ch08 Task 3
수영	swimming	Ch08 Task 3
수영하다	to swim	Ch08 Task 3
수족관	aquarium	Ch06 Task 2, Ch06 Task 3
숙제	homework	Ch02 Task 3, Ch06 Task 1
순두부	soft tofu	Ch03 Task 2
순두부찌개	soft tofu stew	Ch08 Task 2, Ch08 Task 3
쉬다	to take a rest	Ch02 Task 1, Ch03 Task 2
쉽다	to be easy	Ch02 Task 1, Ch07 Task 3
스웨터	sweater	Ch01 Task 1
스케줄	schedule	Ch05 Task 1
스터디 어브로드	study abroad	Ch02 Task 2
스포츠	sports	Ch03 Task 2
시간이 많다	to have a lot of time	Ch03 Task 2
시계	watch, clock	Ch04 Task 2, Ch04 Task 3
시끄럽다	to be noisy	Ch01 Task 1
시작하다	to begin	Ch02 Task 1, Ch02 Task 2, Ch02 Task 3
시청	city hall	Ch07 Task 2
시카고	Chicago	Ch04 Task 2, Ch04 Task 3
시키다	to order	Ch08 Task 2
시험	exam	Ch03 Task 3
식당	restaurant	Ch08 Task 2
식물원	botanical garden	Ch03 Task 3
신기하다	to be miraculous	Ch07 Task 1
신나다	to be excited	Ch01 Task 1, Ch01 Task 3
신발	shoes	Ch06 Task 1
신발을 신다	to wear shoes	Ch06 Task 1
싸다	to be cheap	Ch01 Task 1, Ch03 Task 2
쓰다	to use, write, wear (a hat, glasses)	Ch04 Task 1, Ch04 Task 2, Ch04 Task 3, Ch07 Task 1, Ch07 Task 2, Ch07 Task 3

아

아르바이트하다	to do a part-time job	Ch02 Task 1
아름답다	to be beautiful	Ch01 Task 3, Ch06 Task 2, Ch06 Task 3
아주	very	Ch08 Task 2
아직	yet, still	Ch05 Task 2, Ch05 Task 3
아침	morning	Ch07 Task 2
악기	instrument	Ch05 Task 1
안	inside	Ch02 Task 2, Ch02 Task 3, Ch06 Task 1
아침 식사	breakfast	Ch03 Task 3
아프다	to be sick	Ch05 Task 2, Ch05 Task 3

안경	glasses	Ch04 Task 1, Ch04 Task 2, Ch04 Task 3
앉다	to sit	Ch04 Task 1
알아보다	to search for	Ch03 Task 1
액세서리	accessories	Ch04 Task 3
약	medicine, drugs	Ch05 Task 2, Ch05 Task 3
양복	suit	Ch07 Task 1
어렵다	to be difficult	Ch02 Task 1
어젯밤	last night	Ch03 Task 3
언어	language	Ch02 Task 2, Ch02 Task 3
에스컬레이터	escalator	Ch07 Task 1
여기	here	Ch07 Task 2
여러분	everyone	Ch08 Task 1
여름	summer	Ch02 Task 2, Ch06 Task 1
여자친구	girlfriend	Ch04 Task 3
여행	trip	Ch03 Task 1, Ch04 Task 1
여행하다	to travel	Ch02 Task 1, Ch02 Task 3, Ch06 Task 1, Ch07 Task 1
역	station	Ch07 Task 2
역사	history	Ch02 Task 2, Ch02 Task 3
연구실	professor's office	Ch02 Task 1, Ch02 Task 2
연극	play	Ch03 Task 1
연극표	theater ticket	Ch03 Task 1
연세	age (honorific)	Ch01 Task 1
연습하다	to practice	Ch02 Task 2
영국	England	Ch04 Task 2
영어	English	Ch08 Task 1
영업시간	business hours	Ch03 Task 2
예쁘다	to be pretty	Ch01 Task 2
예약하다	to book, reserve	Ch08 Task 2
오늘	today	Ch03 Task 1
오빠	older brother of a female speaker	Ch05 Task 2, Ch05 Task 3
올라가다	to go up	Ch07 Task 1
올라오다	to come up	Ch07 Task 2
요리 기구	cooking utensils	Ch07 Task 3
요리 수업	cooking class	Ch08 Task 3
요리하다	to cook	Ch03 Task 1, Ch04 Task 2, Ch04 Task 3
요즘	recently	Ch06 Task 2, Ch06 Task 3
우버	Uber	Ch06 Task 2, Ch06 Task 3
운동장	stadium, playground	Ch05 Task 1
원래 가격	original price	Ch07 Task 2
월	month (counter)	Ch01 Task 2
위험하다	to be dangerous	Ch06 Task 2, Ch06 Task 3
유명하다	to be famous	Ch08 Task 2, Ch08 Task 3
음식	food	Ch01 Task 1
음식을 만들다	to make food	Ch01 Task 1, Ch01 Task 2, Ch01 Task 3
음악	music	Ch02 Task 2
의자	chair	Ch08 Task 1
이메일	email	Ch07 Task 2
이번 주말	this weekend	Ch03 Task 1
이번 학기	this semester	Ch02 Task 1, Ch03 Task 1
이번(에)	this time	Ch03 Task 1
이벤트	event	Ch01 Task 1, Ch01 Task 3, Ch05 Task 1
이사하다	to move (to a different place)	Ch04 Task 2, Ch07 Task 2
이야기를 듣다	to hear a story	Ch01 Task 1
(하고) 이야기를 하다	to talk (with)	Ch01 Task 2, Ch01 Task 3, Ch02 Task 1
이유	reason	Ch05 Task 1, Ch05 Task 2, Ch05 Task 3, Ch07 Task 2, Ch08 Task 3
인터뷰	interview	Ch05 Task 1, Ch05 Task 2, Ch05 Task 3
인턴십	internship	Ch05 Task 2, Ch05 Task 3
일	day (counter)	Ch01 Task 2
일어나다	to wake up	Ch04 Task 1
일요일	Sunday	Ch03 Task 1, Ch03 Task 2
일찍	early	Ch02 Task 1, Ch03 Task 2
일하다	to work	Ch02 Task 1

입고 가다	to wear and go	Ch07 Task 1
입다	to wear (clothes)	Ch04 Task 1, Ch04 Task 2, Ch04 Task 3, Ch07 Task 1, Ch07 Task 3, Ch08 Task 3

자

자료	materials	Ch05 Task 2, Ch05 Task 3
자르다	to cut	Ch08 Task 1, Ch08 Task 2
자리	seat	Ch08 Task 2
자전거	bicycle	Ch07 Task 1
자주	often	Ch02 Task 1, Ch02 Task 2, Ch02 Task 3
작다	to be small	Ch01 Task 3, Ch07 Task 3
(을/를) 잘하다	to be good at	Ch02 Task 1, Ch03 Task 2, Ch08 Task 1
장갑	gloves	Ch01 Task 1, Ch04 Task 2, Ch04 Task 3
장소	place	Ch04 Task 2, Ch05 Task 1, Ch08 Task 3
장점	advantages	Ch02 Task 2, Ch02 Task 3
재료	ingredient	Ch05 Task 1
재미없다	to be boring	Ch01 Task 1, Ch01 Task 2, Ch01 Task 3
재미있다	to be fun	Ch01 Task 1, Ch01 Task 2, Ch01 Task 3, Ch06 Task 1
적다	to be little, few	Ch01 Task 1, Ch01 Task 3
전공	major	Ch02 Task 1, Ch02 Task 2, Ch02 Task 3
전공하다	to major in	Ch02 Task 1
전주	Jeonju	Ch08 Task 3
전화번호	phone number	Ch07 Task 2
전화하다	to make a call	Ch03 Task 3
점심	lunch	Ch03 Task 3
젓가락	chopsticks	Ch08 Task 1, Ch08 Task 2
젓가락질	use of chopsticks	Ch08 Task 1
정문	main gate	Ch07 Task 2
제주도	Jeju Island	Ch02 Task 3, Ch06 Task 1
조 모임	group meeting	Ch05 Task 1
졸업식	graduation ceremony	Ch07 Task 1
졸업하다	to graduate	Ch02 Task 1, Ch04 Task 3, Ch07 Task 2
종업원	employee, server	Ch08 Task 1, Ch08 Task 2
좋아하다	to like	Ch08 Task 3
죄송하다	to be sorry	Ch02 Task 1, Ch02 Task 2
주다	to give	Ch06 Task 1
주말	weekend	Ch08 Task 2
주무시다	to sleep (honorific)	Ch01 Task 2
주문하다	to order (food)	Ch08 Task 1, Ch08 Task 2
주시다	to give (honorific)	Ch01 Task 1, Ch01 Task 2, Ch01 Task 3
주차장	parking lot	Ch08 Task 1
주차하다	to park	Ch08 Task 1
주최자	organizer	Ch05 Task 1
(을/를) 준비하다	to prepare for	Ch03 Task 3, Ch05 Task 1, Ch07 Task 3
중간고사	midterm	Ch03 Task 3
중간고사 기간	midterm week	Ch03 Task 3
중식당	Chinese restaurant	Ch08 Task 1, Ch08 Task 2
즐겁다	to be joyful	Ch01 Task 1, Ch01 Task 2, Ch01 Task 3, Ch06 Task 1
지금	now	Ch06 Task 1
지난 주	last week	Ch07 Task 1
지난 학기	last semester	Ch03 Task 3
지내다	to spend (time), live	Ch06 Task 1
(에) 지원하다	to apply	Ch02 Task 2
지하철	subway	Ch06 Task 1, Ch07 Task 1
지하철 역	subway station	Ch07 Task 2
진지	meal (honorific)	Ch01 Task 2
집	house	Ch05 Task 2, Ch05 Task 3
짜장면	jjajangmyeon	Ch08 Task 1
짧다	to be short	Ch01 Task 1, Ch01 Task 2, Ch01 Task 3, Ch06 Task 2, Ch06 Task 3

짬뽕	jjamppong	Ch08 Task 1
쯤	about	Ch07 Task 2

차

차	car	Ch06 Task 2, Ch06 Task 3
차	tea	Ch02 Task 3
차갑다	to be cold	Ch08 Task 2
차다	to be cold, to wear (a belt)	Ch04 Task 2, Ch08 Task 1, Ch08 Task 3
찾다	to look for	Ch03 Task 3
책갈피	bookmark	Ch01 Task 3
처음으로	for the first time	Ch08 Task 2
첫 번째	first	Ch01 Task 2
청바지	blue jeans	Ch03 Task 2
청소하다	to clean	Ch07 Task 1
체험학습	field trip	Ch02 Task 3
추천하다	to recommend	Ch08 Task 2
축제	festival	Ch05 Task 1
출구	exit	Ch07 Task 2
춤	dance	Ch05 Task 1
춤을 추다	to dance	Ch03 Task 1, Ch03 Task 3
춥다	to be cold	Ch01 Task 2, Ch01 Task 3, Ch05 Task 2, Ch05 Task 3
충전하다	to charge	Ch07 Task 1
치마	skirt	Ch04 Task 2, Ch04 Task 3

카

카드	card	Ch01 Task 2, Ch01 Task 3
카드를 쓰다	to write a card	Ch01 Task 1
카메라	camera	Ch07 Task 1
캐나다	Canada	Ch03 Task 1
캐릭터	character	Ch07 Task 3
캠퍼스	campus	Ch02 Task 2, Ch02 Task 3
커피 머신	coffee machine	Ch07 Task 2
커피숍	café	Ch03 Task 3
콘서트	concert	Ch06 Task 1
쿠키	cookies	Ch07 Task 3
크다	to be big	Ch08 Task 1, Ch01 Task 3
크리스마스	Christmas	Ch01 Task 2
크리스마스 트리	Christmas tree	Ch04 Task 2
클럽	club	Ch02 Task 2, Ch02 Task 3, Ch03 Task 3

타

타고 가다	to go riding	Ch07 Task 1
타고 다니다	to ride around	Ch07 Task 1
타다	to ride, get on	Ch06 Task 2, Ch06 Task 3, Ch07 Task 1, Ch07 Task 2
탁자	table	Ch01 Task 3
택시	taxi	Ch02 Task 3, Ch02 Task 2
택시 기사	taxi driver	Ch06 Task 1
택시 요금	taxi fare	Ch06 Task 2, Ch06 Task 3
테이블	table	Ch08 Task 1
토요일	Saturday	Ch03 Task 1, Ch03 Task 2
특징	characteristic	Ch08 Task 2, Ch08 Task 3
티셔츠	T-shirts	Ch04 Task 2, Ch04 Task 3
팁	tip	Ch06 Task 1

파

파랗다	to be blue	Ch04 Task 1, Ch04 Task 2, Ch04 Task 2, Ch04 Task 3
파워포인트	PowerPoint	Ch05 Task 2, Ch05 Task 3
파트너	partner	Ch08 Task 2
파티	party	Ch01 Task 2, Ch07 Task 3
팔다	to sell	Ch07 Task 2
편리하다	to be convenient	Ch07 Task 3
편하다	to be convenient, comfortable	Ch02 Task 2, Ch02 Task 3, Ch08 Task 1

포스터	poster	Ch05 Task 1
표	ticket	Ch06 Task 1
프랑스	France	Ch06 Task 1
프로그램	program	Ch02 Task 2, Ch02 Task 3
(이/가) 필요하다	to be necessary	Ch05 Task 1, Ch07 Task 3

하

하다	to wear (a necktie, accessories)	Ch04 Task 2, Ch04 Task 3
하얗다	to be white	Ch04 Task 1, Ch04 Task 2, Ch04 Task 3
학기	semester	Ch02 Task 2, Ch03 Task 3
학비	tuition	Ch02 Task 2
학생회관	student center	Ch01 Task 3, Ch05 Task 1
한국 문화	Korean culture	Ch01 Task 3
한국 문화 축제	Korean culture festival	Ch06 Task 2, Ch06 Task 3
한복	hanbok (Korean traditional clothes)	Ch05 Task 1, Ch08 Task 3
한식당	Korean restaurant	Ch08 Task 1, Ch08 Task 2
한옥 마을	hanok village	Ch08 Task 3
할리우드	Hollywood	Ch04 Task 1
할인하다	to give a discount	Ch03 Task 2, Ch07 Task 2, Ch07 Task 3
해운대	Haeundae	Ch08 Task 3
행복하다	to be happy	Ch01 Task 3, Ch06 Task 1
헤어밴드	hairband	Ch04 Task 1
형	older brother of a male speaker	Ch05 Task 2, Ch05 Task 3
호텔	hotel	Ch03 Task 1, Ch04 Task 1
혼자	alone	Ch06 Task 2, Ch06 Task 3
회계	treasurer	Ch05 Task 1
회색	gray	Ch04 Task 2, Ch04 Task 3
회장	president (of a club)	Ch05 Task 1

Vocabulary Index 2 (English-Korean)

A

English	Korean	Tasks (Ch -> Chapter)
about	쯤	Ch07 Task 2
accessories	액세서리	Ch04 Task 3
advantages	장점	Ch02 Task 2, Ch02 Task 3
age (honorific)	연세	Ch01 Task 1
airline ticket	비행기표	Ch03 Task 1
airplane	비행기	Ch03 Task 1
alone	혼자	Ch06 Task 2, Ch06 Task 3
apply	(에) 지원하다	Ch02 Task 2
aquarium	수족관	Ch06 Task 2, Ch06 Task 3
at that time	그때	Ch04 Task 2

B

English	Korean	Tasks (Ch -> Chapter)
bag	가방	Ch04 Task 2
be in a traffic jam	길이 막히다	Ch06 Task 2, Ch06 Task 3
beach	바닷가	Ch03 Task 1, Ch04 Task 1, Ch08 Task 3
beautiful	아름답다	Ch01 Task 3, Ch06 Task 2, Ch06 Task 3
begin	시작하다	Ch02 Task 1, Ch02 Task 2, Ch02 Task 3
bibimbap	비빔밥	Ch02 Task 3, Ch08 Task 3
bicycle	자전거	Ch07 Task 1
big	크다	Ch08 Task 1, Ch01 Task 3
biology	생물학	Ch03 Task 3
birthday (honorific)	생신	Ch01 Task 2
black	까맣다	Ch04 Task 1, Ch04 Task 2, Ch04 Task 3, Ch07 Task 1
blocked, congested	길이 막히다	Ch02 Task 1, Ch02 Task 2, Ch02 Task 3
bloom	꽃이 피다	Ch06 Task 2, Ch06 Task 3
blue	파랗다	Ch04 Task 1, Ch04 Task 2, Ch04 Task 2, Ch04 Task 3
blue jeans	청바지	Ch03 Task 2
boarding expenses	기숙사비	Ch02 Task 2
book, reserve	예약하다	Ch08 Task 2
bookmark	책갈피	Ch01 Task 3
booth	부스	Ch01 Task 3
boring	재미없다	Ch01 Task 1, Ch01 Task 2, Ch01 Task 3
borrow	빌리다	Ch05 Task 1
botanical garden	식물원	Ch03 Task 3
bread	빵	Ch07 Task 3
break	깨지다	Ch07 Task 2
breakfast	아침 식사	Ch03 Task 3
bring	갖고 오다	Ch07 Task 1
bring/take something to someone	갖다 드리다	Ch07 Task 2, Ch07 Task 3
building	건물	Ch07 Task 2
bulgogi	불고기	Ch03 Task 1
bus stop	버스 정류장	Ch07 Task 2
Busan	부산	Ch08 Task 3
business hours	영업시간	Ch03 Task 2
busy	바쁘다	Ch06 Task 1, Ch07 Task 2
buy	사다	Ch04 Task 1, Ch04 Task 2, Ch04 Task 3, Ch06 Task 1, Ch07 Task 1, Ch07 Task 2

C

English	Korean	Tasks (Ch -> Chapter)
café	커피숍	Ch03 Task 3
camera	카메라	Ch07 Task 1
campus	캠퍼스	Ch02 Task 2, Ch02 Task 3
Canada	캐나다	Ch03 Task 1
cap, hat	모자	Ch04 Task 2, Ch04 Task 3, Ch06 Task 1
car	차	Ch06 Task 2, Ch06 Task 3

English	Korean	Tasks (Ch -> Chapter)
card	카드	Ch01 Task 2, Ch01 Task 3
carry around	갖고 다니다	Ch07 Task 1
catch a cold	감기에 걸리다	Ch05 Task 2, Ch05 Task 3
Central Park	센트럴파크	Ch04 Task 2
chair	의자	Ch08 Task 1
change	바꾸다	Ch05 Task 1
character	캐릭터	Ch07 Task 3
characteristic	특징	Ch08 Task 2, Ch08 Task 3
charge	충전하다	Ch07 Task 1
cheap	싸다	Ch01 Task 1, Ch03 Task 2
Chicago	시카고	Ch04 Task 2, Ch04 Task 3
chicken galbi	닭갈비	Ch03 Task 2
Chinese restaurant	중식당	Ch08 Task 1, Ch08 Task 2
choose	고르다	Ch07 Task 1
chopsticks	젓가락	Ch08 Task 1, Ch08 Task 2
Christmas	크리스마스	Ch01 Task 2
Christmas tree	크리스마스 트리	Ch04 Task 2
city	도시	Ch04 Task 2, Ch06 Task 1
city hall	시청	Ch07 Task 2
class, lesson	수업	Ch06 Task 1
classroom	교실	Ch06 Task 1
clean	깨끗하다 , 청소하다	Ch02 Task 2, Ch07 Task 1
close	문을 닫다	Ch03 Task 2, Ch03 Task 3
closing time	닫는 시간	Ch03 Task 3
club	클럽	Ch02 Task 2, Ch02 Task 3, Ch03 Task 3
coffee machine	커피 머신	Ch07 Task 2
cold	감기, 차다 , 차갑다, 춥다	Ch01 Task 2, Ch01 Task 3, Ch05 Task 2, Ch05 Task 3, Ch08 Task 1, Ch08 Task 2, Ch08 Task 3
come in	들어오다	Ch07 Task 2
come up	올라오다	Ch07 Task 2
concert	콘서트	Ch06 Task 1
convenient	편리하다	Ch07 Task 3
convenient, comfortable	편하다	Ch02 Task 2, Ch02 Task 3, Ch08 Task 1
cook	요리하다	Ch03 Task 1, Ch04 Task 2, Ch04 Task 3
cookie, snack	과자	Ch07 Task 3
cookies	쿠키	Ch07 Task 3
cooking class	요리 수업	Ch08 Task 3
cooking utensils	요리 기구	Ch07 Task 3
cost	돈이 들다	Ch03 Task 1
cost of living	물가	Ch05 Task 1
counting unit	개	Ch03 Task 3
crowded	사람이 많다, 복잡하다	Ch03 Task 1, Ch02 Task 1, Ch02 Task 2, Ch02 Task 3
culture	문화	Ch02 Task 1, Ch02 Task 2, Ch02 Task 3, Ch06 Task 1, Ch08 Task 3
cut	자르다	Ch08 Task 1, Ch08 Task 2

D

English	Korean	Tasks (Ch -> Chapter)
dance	춤, 춤을 추다	Ch03 Task 1, Ch03 Task 3, Ch05 Task 1
dangerous	위험하다	Ch06 Task 2, Ch06 Task 3
dawn	새벽	Ch03 Task 3
day (counter)	일	Ch01 Task 2
decorate	꾸미다	Ch05 Task 1
delicious	맛있다	Ch01 Task 3, Ch08 Task 1
department store	백화점	Ch04 Task 1
different	(하고) 다르다	Ch06 Task 1, Ch06 Task 2, Ch06 Task 3, Ch08 Task 3
difficult	어렵다	Ch02 Task 1
disadvantages	단점	Ch02 Task 2, Ch02 Task 3
Disneyland	디즈니랜드	Ch04 Task 1
distance	거리	Ch03 Task 1, Ch03 Task 3
do a part-time job	아르바이트하다	Ch02 Task 1

dollar	달러	Ch03 Task 1
dormitory	기숙사	Ch02 Task 1, Ch03 Task 3, Ch07 Task 2
double date	더블 데이트(를 하다)	Ch03 Task 2
drama	드라마	Ch02 Task 1
drink	마시다	Ch03 Task 3
during, for	동안	Ch05 Task 1, Ch07 Task 1

E

early	일찍	Ch02 Task 1, Ch03 Task 2
earring	귀걸이	Ch04 Task 2, Ch04 Task 3
easy	쉽다	Ch02 Task 1, Ch07 Task 3
eat (honorific)	드시다	Ch01 Task 1, Ch01 Task 2, Ch01 Task 3
email	이메일	Ch07 Task 2
employee, server	종업원	Ch08 Task 1, Ch08 Task 2
end	끝나다	Ch04 Task 2
England	영국	Ch04 Task 2
English	영어	Ch08 Task 1
enter	들어가다	Ch07 Task 2
escalator	에스컬레이터	Ch07 Task 1
event	이벤트	Ch01 Task 1, Ch01 Task 3, Ch05 Task 1
everyone	여러분	Ch08 Task 2
exam	시험	Ch03 Task 3
exchange	교환	Ch02 Task 2, Ch02 Task 3
excited	신나다	Ch01 Task 1, Ch01 Task 3
exit	출구	Ch07 Task 2
expensive	비싸다	Ch01 Task 1, Ch01 Task 2, Ch03 Task 2, Ch06 Task 2, Ch06 Task 3, Ch08 Task 3
experience	경험하다	Ch08 Task 3

F

fall, autumn	가을	Ch02 Task 2
famous	유명하다	Ch08 Task 2, Ch08 Task 3
far	멀다	Ch03 Task 2, Ch08 Task 1, Ch08 Task 2
far away	멀리	Ch02 Task 1
fast	빨리, 빠르다	Ch07 Task 3, Ch06 Task 1, Ch07 Task 3
festival	축제	Ch05 Task 1
field trip	체험학습	Ch02 Task 3
final exam	기말고사	Ch06 Task 2, Ch06 Task 3
final exam week	기말고사 기간	Ch06 Task 2, Ch06 Task 3
first	첫 번째	Ch01 Task 2
flower	꽃	Ch04 Task 1, Ch06 Task 2, Ch06 Task 3
food	음식	Ch01 Task 1
for free	공짜로	Ch07 Task 2, Ch07 Task 3
for the first time	처음으로	Ch08 Task 2
France	프랑스	Ch06 Task 1
free	공짜	Ch07 Task 2, Ch07 Task 3
full	다 차다	Ch02 Task 1
fun	재미있다	Ch01 Task 1, Ch01 Task 2, Ch01 Task 3, Ch06 Task 1

G

galbi	갈비	Ch03 Task 1, Ch03 Task 2, Ch08 Task 1, Ch08 Task 2
get a haircut	머리를 자르다	Ch06 Task 2, Ch06 Task 3
get off	내리다	Ch07 Task 2
get something dry cleaned	드라이클리닝을 하다	Ch07 Task 1
girlfriend	여자친구	Ch04 Task 3
give	주다	Ch06 Task 1
give (honorific)	주시다	Ch01 Task 1, Ch01 Task 2, Ch01 Task 3
give (humble)	드리다	Ch01 Task 1, Ch01 Task 2, Ch01 Task 3

give a discount	할인하다	Ch03 Task 2, Ch07 Task 2, Ch07 Task 3
glasses	안경	Ch04 Task 1, Ch04 Task 2, Ch04 Task 3
gloves	장갑	Ch01 Task 1, Ch04 Task 2, Ch04 Task 3
go	가다	Ch04 Task 2, Ch04 Task 3
go to church	교회에 가다	Ch03 Task 1
go down	내려오다	Ch07 Task 1
go on foot	걸어가다	Ch07 Task 1
go riding	타고 가다	Ch07 Task 1
go shopping	쇼핑하다	Ch04 Task 2, Ch07 Task 1
go up	올라가다	Ch07 Task 1
golf	골프	Ch03 Task 1
good at	(을/를) 잘하다	Ch02 Task 1, Ch03 Task 2, Ch08 Task 1
GoPro	고프로	Ch07 Task 1, Ch07 Task 3
graduate	졸업하다	Ch02 Task 1, Ch04 Task 3, Ch07 Task 2
graduation ceremony	졸업식	Ch07 Task 1
gray	회색	Ch04 Task 2, Ch04 Task 3
group meeting	조 모임	Ch05 Task 1
guesthouse	게스트하우스	Ch08 Task 3

H

Haeundae	해운대	Ch08 Task 3
hairband	헤어밴드	Ch04 Task 1
hanbok (Korean traditional clothes)	한복	Ch05 Task 1, Ch08 Task 3
handwriting	글씨	Ch05 Task 1
hanok village	한옥 마을	Ch08 Task 3
happy	행복하다	Ch01 Task 3, Ch06 Task 1
have a lot of time	시간이 많다	Ch03 Task 2
head, hair	머리	Ch05 Task 2, Ch05 Task 3, Ch06 Task 2, Ch06 Task 3
hear a story	이야기를 듣다	Ch01 Task 1
help	돕다	Ch05 Task 2, Ch05 Task 3
here	여기	Ch07 Task 2
high school	고등학교	Ch04 Task 2
history	역사	Ch02 Task 2, Ch02 Task 3
Hollywood	할리우드	Ch04 Task 1
homework	숙제	Ch02 Task 3, Ch06 Task 1
hot	덥다	Ch01 Task 3, Ch06 Task 1
hotel	호텔	Ch03 Task 1, Ch04 Task 1
house	집	Ch05 Task 2, Ch05 Task 3
house (honorific)	댁	Ch01 Task 1, Ch01 Task 2, Ch05 Task 2, Ch05 Task 3

I / J / K

in advance	미리	Ch08 Task 2
inconvenient, uncomfortable	불편하다	Ch02 Task 1, Ch02 Task 2, Ch02 Task 3, Ch08 Task 1
ingredient	재료	Ch05 Task 1
inside	안	Ch02 Task 2, Ch02 Task 3, Ch06 Task 1
instrument	악기	Ch05 Task 1
international	국제	Ch02 Task 2, Ch02 Task 3
internship	인턴십	Ch05 Task 2, Ch05 Task 3
interview	인터뷰	Ch05 Task 1, Ch05 Task 2, Ch05 Task 3
introduce	소개하다	Ch01 Task 2, Ch05 Task 1
Jeju Island	제주도	Ch02 Task 3, Ch06 Task 1
Jeonju	전주	Ch08 Task 3
jjajangmyeon	짜장면	Ch08 Task 1
jjamppong	짬뽕	Ch08 Task 1
job interview	면접	Ch07 Task 1
joyful	즐겁다	Ch01 Task 1, Ch01 Task 2, Ch01 Task 3, Ch06 Task 1
kimchi	김치	Ch02 Task 2
Korean culture	한국 문화	Ch01 Task 3
Korean culture festival	한국 문화 축제	Ch06 Task 2, Ch06 Task 3

Korean restaurant	한식당	Ch08 Task 1, Ch08 Task 2

L

lab	랩	Ch03 Task 3
language	언어	Ch02 Task 2, Ch02 Task 3
last night	어젯밤	Ch03 Task 3
last semester	지난 학기	Ch03 Task 3
last week	지난 주	Ch07 Task 3
late	늦다, 늦게	Ch02 Task 1, Ch02 Task 2, Ch02 Task 3, Ch03 Task 2, Ch06 Task 2, Ch06 Task 3
late for class	수업에 늦다	Ch02 Task 1
learn	배우다	Ch02 Task 1, Ch02 Task 3, Ch08 Task 1, Ch08 Task 3
lend	빌려주다	Ch05 Task 1
library	도서관	Ch03 Task 3
like	좋아하다	Ch08 Task 3
little, few	적다	Ch01 Task 1, Ch01 Task 3
live	살다	Ch06 Task 1
long	길다	Ch01 Task 1, Ch01 Task 2, Ch01 Task 3, Ch06 Task 2, Ch06 Task 3, Ch08 Task 1, Ch08 Task 2, Ch08 Task 3
look for	찾다	Ch03 Task 3
Los Angeles	로스 앤젤레스	Ch04 Task 1
lunch	점심	Ch03 Task 3

M

main gate	정문	Ch07 Task 2
major	전공	Ch02 Task 1, Ch02 Task 2, Ch02 Task 3
major in	전공하다	Ch02 Task 1
make	만들다	Ch02 Task 3, Ch03 Task 1, Ch04 Task 2, Ch04 Task 3, Ch07 Task 2, Ch07 Task 3, Ch08 Task 3
make a call	전화하다	Ch03 Task 3
make food	음식을 만들다	Ch01 Task 1, Ch01 Task 2, Ch01 Task 3
many, much	많다	Ch01 Task 1, Ch01 Task 3
marry	결혼하다	Ch04 Task 2, Ch04 Task 3, Ch05 Task 2, Ch05 Task 3
materials	자료	Ch05 Task 2, Ch05 Task 3
meal (honorific)	진지	Ch01 Task 2
medicine, drugs	약	Ch05 Task 2, Ch05 Task 3
meet	만나다	Ch04 Task 1, Ch04 Task 2, Ch04 Task 3, Ch06 Task 2, Ch06 Task 3
menu	메뉴	Ch02 Task 2, Ch02 Task 3
Mickey Mouse	미키	Ch04 Task 1
midterm	중간고사	Ch03 Task 3
midterm week	중간고사 기간	Ch03 Task 3
milmyeon	밀면	Ch08 Task 3
mini-oven	미니오븐	Ch07 Task 3
Minnie Mouse	미니	Ch04 Task 1
minute	분	Ch07 Task 2
miraculous	신기하다	Ch07 Task 1
money	돈	Ch05 Task 1
month (counter)	월	Ch01 Task 2
morning	아침	Ch07 Task 2
move (to a different place)	이사하다	Ch04 Task 2, Ch07 Task 2
music	음악	Ch02 Task 2

N

naengmyeon	냉면	Ch08 Task 1, Ch08 Task 2, Ch08 Task 3
name (honorific)	성함	Ch01 Task 1
near	가깝다	Ch03 Task 2, Ch08 Task 1
necessary	(이/가) 필요하다	Ch05 Task 1, Ch07 Task 3

neck, throat	목	Ch05 Task 2, Ch05 Task 3
necklace	목걸이	Ch04 Task 2, Ch04 Task 3
necktie	넥타이	Ch04 Task 2, Ch04 Task 3
New York	뉴욕	Ch04 Task 2
next semester	다음 학기	Ch02 Task 1
next time	다음 번	Ch08 Task 2
nice	멋지다	Ch01 Task 2, Ch01 Task 3
night	밤	Ch06 Task 2, Ch06 Task 3
noisy	시끄럽다	Ch01 Task 1
noodle	면	Ch08 Task 1, Ch08 Task 2, Ch08 Task 3
noraebang	노래방	Ch02 Task 3, Ch06 Task 2, Ch06 Task 3
not know	모르다	Ch06 Task 2, Ch06 Task 3
not know how to get somewhere	길을 모르다	Ch06 Task 2, Ch06 Task 3
now	지금	Ch06 Task 1

O

office hours	면담 시간	Ch05 Task 1
often	자주	Ch02 Task 1, Ch02 Task 2, Ch02 Task 3
older brother of a female speaker	오빠	Ch05 Task 2, Ch05 Task 3
older brother of a male speaker	형	Ch05 Task 2, Ch05 Task 3
open	문을 열다	Ch03 Task 2
order	시키다	Ch08 Task 2
order (food)	주문하다	Ch08 Task 1, Ch08 Task 2
organizer	주최자	Ch05 Task 1
original price	원래 가격	Ch07 Task 2
outside	밖	Ch02 Task 1, Ch02 Task 2, Ch02 Task 3

P

pants	바지	Ch04 Task 2, Ch04 Task 3
parents	부모님	Ch05 Task 2, Ch05 Task 3
park	공원, 주차하다	Ch03 Task 1, Ch06 Task 1, Ch08 Task 1
parking lot	주차장	Ch08 Task 1
partner	파트너	Ch08 Task 2
party	파티	Ch01 Task 2, Ch07 Task 3
people	사람들	Ch01 Task 1
period, term	기간	Ch02 Task 2
phone number	전화번호	Ch07 Task 2
picture	사진	Ch05 Task 2, Ch05 Task 3
picture/drawing	그림	Ch01 Task 3
place	곳, 장소	Ch04 Task 2, Ch05 Task 1, Ch08 Task 3
plan	계획	Ch03 Task 2
play	연극	Ch03 Task 1
play golf	골프를 치다	Ch03 Task 1
play, hang out	놀다	Ch02 Task 1, Ch02 Task 2, Ch02 Task 3, Ch08 Task 3
pork belly	삼겹살	Ch03 Task 2
poster	포스터	Ch05 Task 1
PowerPoint	파워포인트	Ch05 Task 2, Ch05 Task 3
practice	연습하다	Ch02 Task 2
prepare for	(을/를) 준비하다	Ch03 Task 3, Ch05 Task 1, Ch07 Task 3
present, gift	선물	Ch01 Task 1
presentation	발표	Ch05 Task 2, Ch05 Task 3
president (of a club)	회장	Ch05 Task 1
pretty	예쁘다	Ch01 Task 2
price	가격	Ch03 Task 1, Ch03 Task 2, Ch07 Task 2, Ch07 Task 3
professor	교수님	Ch01 Task 3, Ch02 Task 1, Ch02 Task 2, Ch02 Task 3, Ch05 Task 2, Ch05 Task 3
professor's office	연구실	Ch02 Task 1, Ch02 Task 2
program	프로그램	Ch02 Task 2, Ch02 Task 3

put (a poster) on	붙이다	Ch05 Task 1

R

rain	비가 오다	Ch03 Task 1
reason	이유	Ch05 Task 1, Ch05 Task 2, Ch05 Task 3, Ch07 Task 2, Ch08 Task 3
recently	요즘	Ch06 Task 2, Ch06 Task 3
reception	결혼 축하 파티	Ch05 Task 2, Ch05 Task 3
recommend	추천하다	Ch08 Task 2
recover	낫다	Ch05 Task 2, Ch05 Task 3
red	빨갛다	Ch04 Task 1, Ch04 Task 2, Ch04 Task 3
resort	리조트	Ch03 Task 1
restaurant	식당	Ch08 Task 2
reunion	동창회	Ch04 Task 2, Ch04 Task 3
rice cake	떡	Ch01 Task 3, Ch02 Task 3
rice cake soup	떡국	Ch01 Task 1
ride around	타고 다니다	Ch07 Task 1
ride, get on	타다	Ch06 Task 2, Ch06 Task 3, Ch07 Task 1, Ch07 Task 2
ring	반지	Ch04 Task 1, Ch04 Task 2, Ch04 Task 3
roommate	룸메이트	Ch02 Task 1, Ch02 Task 2, Ch02 Task 3, Ch05 Task 2, Ch05 Task 3, Ch06 Task 1

S

samullori (traditional Korean instrumental music)	사물놀이	Ch06 Task 1
sand festival	모래 축제	Ch08 Task 3
sandcastle	모래성	Ch04 Task 1
sandwich	샌드위치	Ch03 Task 3
Santa Claus	산타클로스	Ch04 Task 2
Saturday	토요일	Ch03 Task 1, Ch03 Task 2
schedule	스케줄	Ch05 Task 1
scissors	가위	Ch08 Task 2
search for	알아보다	Ch03 Task 1
seat	자리	Ch08 Task 2
second	두 번째	Ch01 Task 2
see	보다	Ch06 Task 2, Ch06 Task 3, Ch07 Task 2
see (honorific)	뵙다	Ch05 Task 1
sell	팔다	Ch07 Task 2
semester	학기	Ch02 Task 2, Ch03 Task 3
send	보내다	Ch05 Task 1, Ch07 Task 2
Seoul	서울	Ch06 Task 1
shirts	셔츠	Ch04 Task 1, Ch04 Task 2, Ch04 Task 3
shoes	신발	Ch06 Task 1
short	짧다	Ch01 Task 1, Ch01 Task 2, Ch01 Task 3, Ch06 Task 2, Ch06 Task 3
sick	아프다	Ch05 Task 2, Ch05 Task 3
sightsee	구경하다	Ch07 Task 1, Ch08 Task 3
sing a song	노래하다 , 노래를 부르다	Ch02 Task 3, Ch06 Task 1, Ch06 Task 2, Ch06 Task 3
singer	가수	Ch06 Task 2, Ch06 Task 3
sit	앉다	Ch04 Task 1
skirt	치마	Ch04 Task 2, Ch04 Task 3
sleep (honorific)	주무시다	Ch01 Task 2
small	작다	Ch01 Task 3, Ch07 Task 3
snow	눈이 오다	Ch03 Task 1, Ch03 Task 2, Ch04 Task 2
soft tofu	순두부	Ch03 Task 2
soft tofu stew	순두부찌개	Ch08 Task 2, Ch08 Task 3
song	노래	Ch06 Task 1, Ch06 Task 2, Ch06 Task 3
sorry	죄송하다	Ch02 Task 1, Ch02 Task 2
spacious	넓다	Ch08 Task 1

spend (time), live	지내다	Ch06 Task 1
spicy	맵다	Ch02 Task 3, Ch03 Task 2, Ch08 Task 1, Ch08 Task 2, Ch08 Task 3
sports	스포츠	Ch03 Task 2
spring	봄	Ch06 Task 2, Ch06 Task 3
spring break	봄방학	Ch03 Task 1
stadium, playground	운동장	Ch05 Task 1
stairs	계단	Ch07 Task 2
station	역	Ch07 Task 2
store	가게	Ch04 Task 2
student center	학생회관	Ch01 Task 3, Ch05 Task 1
study abroad	스터디 어브로드	Ch02 Task 2
subject	과목	Ch02 Task 1, Ch02 Task 2, Ch02 Task 3
subway	지하철	Ch06 Task 1, Ch07 Task 1
subway station	지하철 역	Ch07 Task 2
suit	양복	Ch07 Task 1
summer	여름	Ch02 Task 2, Ch06 Task 1
Sunday	일요일	Ch03 Task 1, Ch03 Task 2
sunglasses	선글라스	Ch04 Task 1, Ch04 Task 3
sweater	스웨터	Ch01 Task 1
sweet	달다	Ch08 Task 1, Ch08 Task 3
swim	수영하다	Ch08 Task 3
swimming	수영	Ch08 Task 3

T

T-shirts	티셔츠	Ch04 Task 2, Ch04 Task 3
table	탁자, 테이블	Ch01 Task 3, Ch08 Task 1
take	갖고 가다	Ch07 Task 1, Ch07 Task 2, Ch07 Task 3
take (time)	걸리다	Ch03 Task 1
take a class	수업을 듣다	Ch02 Task 1, Ch08 Task 3
take a picture	사진을 찍다	Ch01 Task 1, Ch01 Task 2, Ch01 Task 3, Ch03 Task 1, Ch04 Task 1, Ch05 Task 2, Ch05 Task 3, Ch07 Task 1
take a rest	쉬다	Ch02 Task 1, Ch03 Task 2
talk (with)	(하고) 이야기를 하다	Ch01 Task 2, Ch01 Task 3, Ch02 Task 1
taste	맛	Ch03 Task 2, Ch08 Task 2
taste bad	맛없다	Ch01 Task 3
taxi	택시	Ch02 Task 3, Ch02 Task 2
taxi driver	택시 기사	Ch06 Task 1
taxi fare	택시 요금	Ch06 Task 2, Ch06 Task 3
tea	차	Ch02 Task 3
teach	가르치다	Ch02 Task 3, Ch06 Task 1
text message	문자 메시지	Ch07 Task 2
theater ticket	연극표	Ch03 Task 1
thing, item	물건	Ch07 Task 1
this semester	이번 학기	Ch02 Task 1, Ch03 Task 3
this time	이번(에)	Ch03 Task 1
this weekend	이번 주말	Ch03 Task 2
ticket	표	Ch06 Task 1
tip	팁	Ch06 Task 1
today	오늘	Ch03 Task 1
transportation	교통	Ch02 Task 1, Ch02 Task 2, Ch02 Task 3
travel	여행하다	Ch02 Task 1, Ch02 Task 3, Ch06 Task 1, Ch07 Task 1
treasurer	회계	Ch05 Task 1
trip	여행	Ch03 Task 1, Ch04 Task 1
tuition	학비	Ch02 Task 2
TV station	방송국	Ch06 Task 2, Ch06 Task 3

U/V/W/Y

U.S.	미국	Ch06 Task 2, Ch06 Task 3
Uber	우버	Ch06 Task 2, Ch06 Task 3
university	대학교	Ch06 Task 1, Ch07 Task 2
use of chopsticks	젓가락질	Ch08 Task 1

use, write, wear (a hat, glasses)	쓰다	Ch04 Task 1, Ch04 Task 2, Ch04 Task 3, Ch07 Task 1, Ch07 Task 2, Ch07 Task 3
usually	보통	Ch03 Task 1, Ch03 Task 2
very	아주	Ch08 Task 2
very much	굉장히	Ch02 Task 1, Ch02 Task 2, Ch02 Task 3
wait	기다리다	Ch08 Task 2
wake up	일어나다	Ch04 Task 1
walk	걷다	Ch06 Task 2, Ch06 Task 3, Ch07 Task 2
walk around	걸어다니다	Ch07 Task 1
warm	따뜻하다	Ch01 Task 1, Ch06 Task 2, Ch06 Task 3
watch, clock	시계	Ch04 Task 2, Ch04 Task 3
wear (a belt)	차다	Ch04 Task 2
wear (a necktie, accessories)	하다	Ch04 Task 2, Ch04 Task 3
wear (a necktie)	매다	Ch04 Task 1, Ch04 Task 2, Ch04 Task 3
wear (clothes)	입다	Ch04 Task 1, Ch04 Task 2, Ch04 Task 3, Ch07 Task 1, Ch07 Task 2, Ch07 Task 3, Ch08 Task 3
wear (gloves, a ring, glasses)	끼다	Ch04 Task 1, Ch04 Task 2, Ch04 Task 3
wear a cap	모자를 쓰다	Ch06 Task 1
wear and go	입고 가다	Ch07 Task 1
wear shoes	신발을 신다	Ch06 Task 1
weather	날씨	Ch01 Task 2, Ch01 Task 3, Ch03 Task 1
wedding ceremony	결혼식	Ch05 Task 2, Ch05 Task 3, Ch07 Task 1
weekend	주말	Ch08 Task 2
white	하얗다	Ch04 Task 1, Ch04 Task 2, Ch04 Task 3
windy	바람이 불다	Ch03 Task 1
work	일하다	Ch02 Task 1
write a card	카드를 쓰다	Ch01 Task 1
yellow	노랗다	Ch04 Task 1, Ch04 Task 2, Ch04 Task 3
yet, still	아직	Ch05 Task 2, Ch05 Task 3
younger brother	남동생	Ch03 Task 1

Task Worksheets

Chapter 01
Task 1

Write a Post about a Korean Lunar New Year (설날) Event You Attended

Collaborative Speaking & Writing

Student Names: &

▶ **Include the following information in your post:**
- Where and when the event was held
  - When: Friday, February 13th, and Saturday, February 14th
  - Where: 한인회관 (Korean community center)
- Information about your Korean friend's grandmother
- Description of what you, your partner, and other people did during the event
- Description of your and your partner's impression of the event

> **NOTES**
>
> *(1) Feel free to change the order of the information listed above.*
>
> *(2) Organize your post coherently.*
>
> *(3) Add more information if you have time.*

Home
Announcements
Syllabus
Attendance
Assignments
Files
Discussions
Quizzes
Grades
People

Topic Title

B *I* <u>U</u> A ▾ A ▾ I_x ≡ ≡ ≡ ≡ ≡ x² x₂ ☰ ☰
⊞ ▾ 🔗 ✨ 🖼 Font Sizes ▾ Paragraph ▾

저희는 _____ 하고 _____ 입니다.

_____

_____

_____

_____

_____

_____

_____

_____

_____

_____

_____

_____

_____

_____

_____

_____

_____

_____

_____

_____

_____

_____

Chapter 01
Task 2

Write a Post about Memorable Events

Individual Writing

Student Name:

▶ **Include the following information in your post:**

• Personal introduction

• Introduction of two memorable events

• When and where the events were held

• What you and other people did at the events

• Your impression of the events

• Closing

NOTES

(1) Feel free to change the order of the information listed above.

(2) Organize your post coherently.

(3) Add more information if you have time.

Home
Announcements
Syllabus
Attendance
Assignments
Files
Discussions
Quizzes
Grades
People

Topic Title

B *I* U A ▾ **A** ▾ I_x ≡ ≡ ≡ ≡ ≡ x² x₂ ≡ ≡
⊞ ▾ 🔗 ⌁ 🖼 Font Sizes ▾ Paragraph ▾

제 이름은 _____입니다.

지금부터 기억에 남는(memorable) 두 이벤트를 소개할 거예요.

첫 번째 이벤트는 _____

_____

_____

_____

_____

_____

_____

_____

_____

_____

_____

_____

_____

_____

_____

두 번째 이벤트는 _____

_____

_____

_____

_____

_____

_____

Create a Podcast about a Korean Cultural Event
Individual Speaking

Student Name:

▶ **Include the following information in your podcast:**

- Personal introduction
- Introduction of the cultural event that you attended
- When and where the event was held
- What was at the event site
- What you and other people did at the event
- Your impression of the event
- Closing

NOTES

(1) *Feel free to change the order of the information listed above.*

(2) *Organize your podcast coherently.*

(3) *Add more information if you have time.*

Chapter 01
Task 4:
Real World Task

Make a Presentation to Introduce a Memorable Family Event
Individual Speaking

Student Name:

▶Include the following information in your presentation:

- Personal introduction
- Information about your family event (e.g., time, place, people, decorations, etc.)
- What you and other people did at the event
- Your impressions of the event
- Closing

NOTES

(1) Feel free to change the order of the information listed above.

(2) Organize your presentation coherently.

(3) Add more information if you have time.

Chapter 02
Task 1

Request an Override in a Korean Class

Individual Writing

Student Name:

▶ **Include the following information in your email:**
- Personal introduction
- Why you want to study Korean
- Why you want to request an override
- Closing

NOTES

(1) Organize your email coherently.

(2) Add more information if you have time.

New message

To: Show BCC

CC:

Subject: Plain Text

교수님께

안녕하세요. 저는 _____입니다.

_____

_____

_____

_____

_____

_____

_____

_____

_____

_____

_____

_____

_____

_____

_____

_____

_____

_____

_____

Apply for a Korean Study Abroad Program

Collaborative Speaking & Writing

Student Names: &

▶ Include the following information in your email (You MUST include the underlined information on your task sheet):
- Your name and your partner's name
- The purpose of the email and a total of <u>four reasons</u> why you and your partner want to study abroad in Korea
- <u>At least two pieces of information</u> about the program and the dormitory from each program (a total of four)
- The program that you and your partner want to attend together
- Two advantages of the program that you want to attend with two respective disadvantages of the program that you do NOT want to attend (i.e., compare the two programs by presenting two advantages motivating you to choose that program and two disadvantages that explain why you would avoid the other program)
- Closing

NOTES

(1) Feel free to change the order of the information listed above.

(2) Organize your email coherently.

(3) Add more information if you have time.

New message   _ ↗ ✕

To:		Show BCC
CC:		
Subject:		Plain Text

교수님께

안녕하세요. 저는 _____하고 _____입니다.

_____

_____

_____

_____

_____

_____

_____

_____

_____

_____

_____

_____

_____

_____

_____

_____

_____

_____

_____

Send

Present Study Abroad Program Experiences to Your Korean Professor
Collaborative Speaking

Student Names: &

▶ Include the following information in your video message:

- Greetings and a statement saying that you and your partner are currently participating in the study abroad program in Korea
- Introduction of two friends that you met and two friends that your partner met while showing pictures that you and your friend took last week
- Description of at least two good things and two bad things about you and your partner's study abroad experiences so far (a total of eight)
- A total of four things that you and your partner want to do next week
- Closing

NOTES

(1) Feel free to change the order of the information listed above.

(2) Organize your video message coherently.

(3) Add more information if you have time.

Write an Email to Your Korean Professor

Individual Writing

Student Name:

▶ **Include the following information in your email:**
- Personal introduction
- Why you are taking the course
- What you like about the course
- What you want to do after learning Korean
- What you want to learn from the course
- Suggestions for improving the course
- What you want to say to the professor
- Closing

NOTES

(1) *Feel free to change the order of the information listed above.*

(2) *Organize your email coherently.*

(3) *Add more information if you have time.*

New message

To: Show BCC

CC:

Subject: Plain Text

교수님께

안녕하세요. 저는 ____________________입니다.

Send

Chapter 03
Task 1

Text a Friend about Spring Break

Collaborative Speaking & Writing

Student Names: &

▶ **Include the following information in your text messages:**
- Opening with questions and answers about what you, your partner, and their parents are doing
- Three things about student A's trip (e.g., weather, how s/he went to the beach)
- Three things about student B's trip (e.g., weather, how s/he went to Canada)
- Decision about what to do for the upcoming weekend

NOTES

(1) Feel free to change the order of the information listed above.

(2) Create your text message exchanges naturally.

(3) Add more information if you have time.

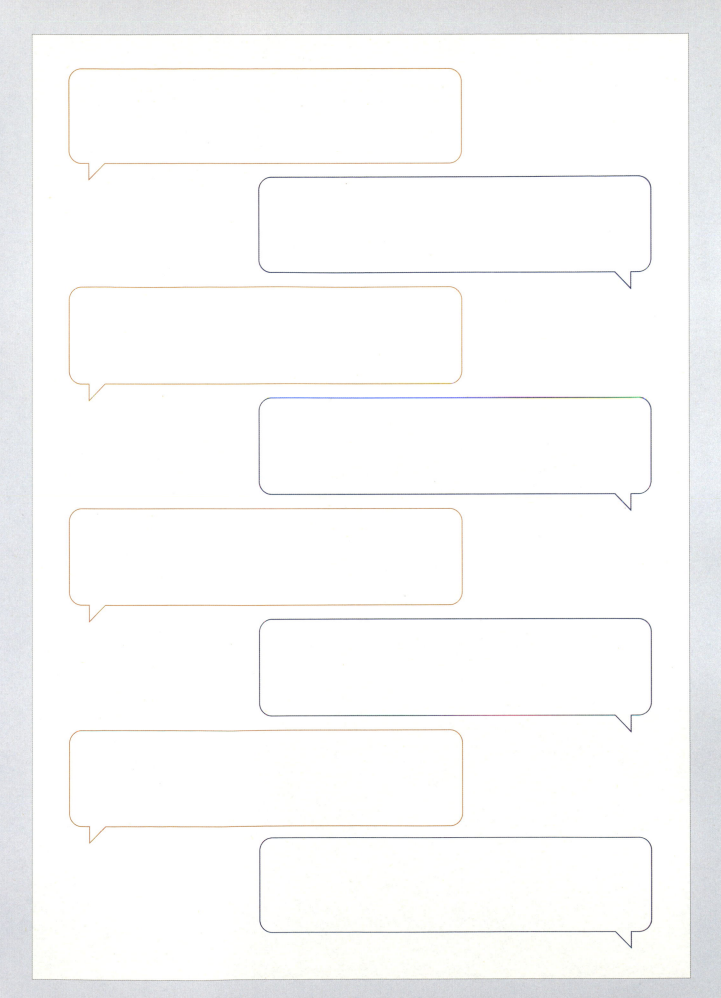

Chapter 03
Task 2

Text a Friend to Plan a Double Date

Collaborative Speaking & Writing

Student Names: &

▶ **Include the following information in the text messages:**
- Opening, asking what student A and B and their boy/girlfriends are doing at the time of texting
- Discussion about the weather during the weekend and when you want to go on a date
- Suggestion for and decision about an activity based on two factors: weather and what couples want to do
- Restaurant details (e.g., distance), to decide which one to go to
- Menu items you and your partner want to have at the restaurant

NOTES

(1) Feel free to change the order of the information listed above.

(2) Create your text message exchanges naturally.

(3) Add more information if you have time.

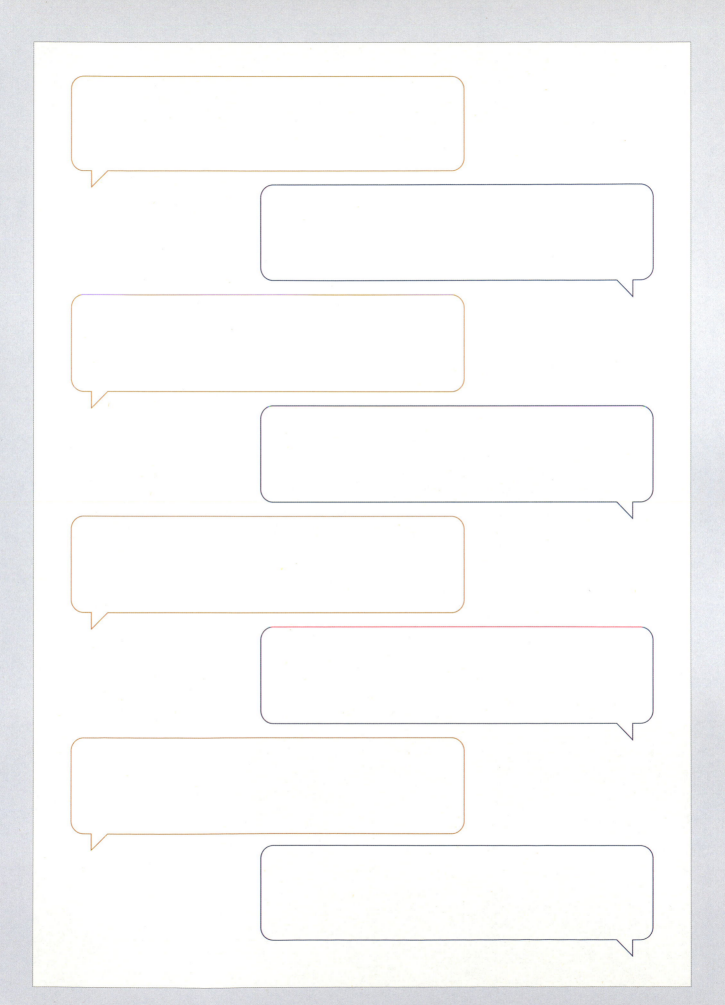

Student Names: &

▶ **Include the following information in the text messages:**

• An opening, asking what students A and B are doing
• Exchange of midterm schedule (e.g., the number of exams or presentations)
• Suggestion to have a study session together for the midterm exams
• Discussion about when you and your partner would like to have a study session tomorrow, considering both students' schedules
• Discussion about where you and your partner want to have the study session while comparing information about the library and café
• Decision of when, for how long, and where you will have a study session together
• Plans after the midterm exams

NOTES

(1) Feel free to change the order of the information listed above.
(2) Create your text message exchanges naturally.
(3) Add more information if you have time.

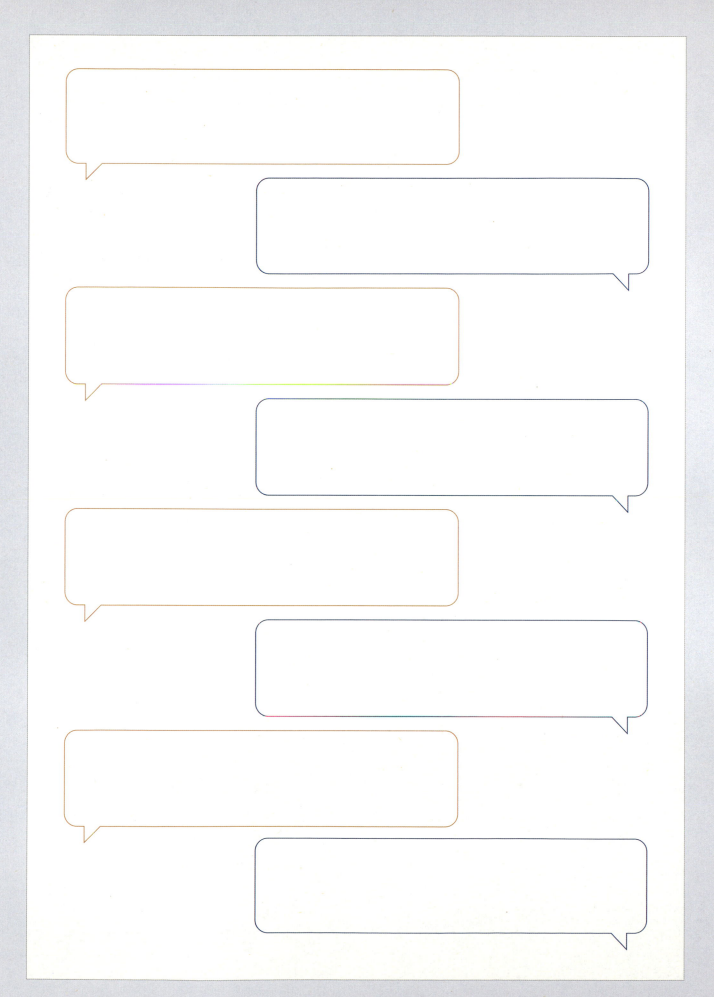

Text a Friend to Make Plans for the Weekend
Collaborative Writing

Student Names: &

▶ **Include the following information in the text messages:**
- An opening, asking what your friend is doing now
- Exchange of weekend schedules
- What you want to do together for the weekend
- Suggestion of when you and your friend would like to meet, considering each other's schedule
- Suggestion of several places you want to meet each other and decide on the best place after considering pros and cons

---

NOTES

(1) Feel free to change the order of the information listed above.

(2) Create your text message exchanges naturally.

(3) Add more information if you have time.

Chapter 04
Task 1

Write a Social Media Post about a Family Trip
Individual Writing

Student Name:

▶ **Share your experience on social media:**
- Introduction of your family trip
- Description of what your family members did in the morning on Day 1 in Hollywood
- Description of what Santa Monica Beach was like and what you and your grandma did in the afternoon on Day 1
- Description of what Disneyland was like and what your mom and brother did there on Day 2

▶ **Comment on other people's posts about their family trips**

NOTES

(1) Organize your post coherently.

(2) Add more information if you have time.

Status Photo Place Life Event

Friends ▼ Post

Comment on Other People's Posts

마이클: 지난 주말에 스키(ski)를 타러 갔는데 눈(snow)이 정말 많이 왔어요.

 Like   Comment

Write a comment...

스티브: 주말에 여행 갔는데 차가 너무 막혔어요.

 Like   Comment

Write a comment...

Chapter 04
Task 2

Write a Social Media Post about Your High School Reunion
Collaborative Speaking & Writing

Student Names: &

▶ **Include the following information in your post:**
- Introduction of two friends whom you and your partner met
  - Description of their clothes and accessories including color
  - Description of what those two friends have been doing since high school graduation
- Description of what you and your partner wore at the high school reunion
- A total of at least 10 things that you and your partner did at the high school reunion

▶ **Comment on other people's posts**

NOTES

(1) Feel free to change the order of the information listed above.

(2) Organize your post coherently.

(3) Add more information if you have time.

Comment on Other People's Posts

소피아: 지난 일요일에 고등학교 친구들하고 센트럴 파크(Central Park)에 **가서** 스케이트(skate)를 탔어요.

 Like 💬 Comment

Write a comment...

미나: 지난 주말에 동창회가 끝나고 예쁜 가방을 샀어요.

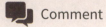 Like 💬 Comment

Write a comment...

Chapter 04
Task 3

Post a Video on Social Media about Your High School Friends
Individual Speaking

Student Name:

▶ **Include the following information in your video:**
- Greetings
- Introduction of the high school reunion and yourself
- Introduction of at least three friends from your picture
  - Description of their clothes and accessories including color
  - Description of their experiences, focusing on what they have been doing since high school graduation
- Closing
- Closing remark:
  "다음은 우리가 같이 한 액티비티를 얘기할 거예요."

NOTES

(1) Feel free to change the order of the information listed above.

(2) Organize your video coherently.

(3) Add more information if you have time.

Comment on Other People's Posts

마이클: 동창회에 갔는데 음식이 아주 많았어요!

 Like   Comment

Write a comment...

스티브: 동창회에 가서 술(alcoholic drink)을 너무 많이 마셨어요.

 Like   Comment

Write a comment...

Chapter 04
Task 4:
Real World Task

Write a Social Media Post about a Memorable Event
Individual Writing

Student Name:

▶ **Include the information below in your writing:**
- Statement of what the event was about
- Introduction of at least four people in the picture(s)
  - Description of their clothes and accessories including color
  - Description of an interesting life event that each person experienced in the past
    (e.g., My sister went to Europe and participated in a study abroad program ➔ 제 여동생은 유럽에 가서 스터디 어브로드를 했어요.)
- Description of what you and other people did at the event
- Description of how you and other people felt about the event

---

NOTES

(1) Feel free to change the order of the information listed above.

(2) Organize your post coherently.

(3) Add more information if you have time.

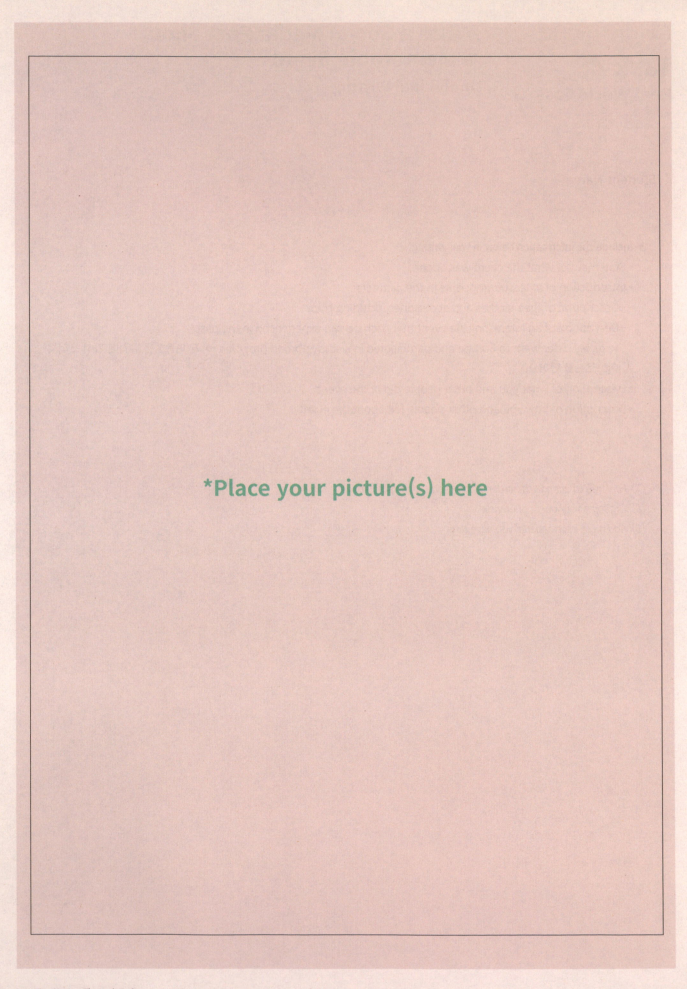

*Place your picture(s) here

Status Photo Place 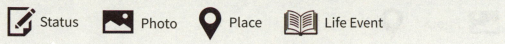 Life Event

Chapter 05
Task 1

Talk on the Phone to Plan Korean Cultural Festival Events
Collaborative Speaking

Student Names: &

▶Include the following information in your phone conversation:
• Greetings on the phone
• Why you are calling
• Events that you and your partner suggest including in the Korean cultural festival
• Things that your club members must do for these events
• Reasons why you would like to change the site
• Reasons why your partner would like to request more money
• When you and your partner would like to visit the festival organizer
• Who will buy the gifts for the students, who will borrow hanbok and instruments, and who will prepare the ingredients for the Korean food
• Closing on the phone

NOTES

(1) Organize your phone conversation naturally.
(2) Use phone expressions as much as possible.
(3) Add more information if you have time.

Chapter 05
Task 2

Talk on the Phone to Discuss Changing a Presentation Date

Collaborative Speaking

Student Names: &

▶Include the following information in your phone conversation:
- Greetings on the phone
- Why you are calling
- All the reasons why you and your partner want to change the presentation date
- Suggestion for a new date when you want to do the presentation and the reason why you can't do the presentation on the suggested date
- Final decision of the date
- Who will call the professor to ask to change the presentation date
- Who will make the PowerPoint and who will prepare the other presentation materials
- Closing on the phone

NOTES

(1) Organize your phone conversation naturally.
(2) Use phone expressions as much as possible.
(3) Add more information if you have time.

Leave a Voicemail Message to Request a Change in Presentation Date
Individual Speaking

Student Name:

▶Include the following information in your message:
- Greetings on the phone
- Why you are calling
- Asking the professor to change the presentation date
- All the reasons why you and your partner cannot make the presentation on the scheduled date (with detailed information)
- Suggestion for the date when you and your partner want to do the presentation
- Two closing sentences that indicate that you and your partner will send the PowerPoint slides via email and that you and your partner will work hard
- Closing on the phone: "그럼, 나중에 다시 전화 드리겠습니다."

NOTES

(1) Organize your voicemail message naturally.
(2) Add more information if you have time.

Leave a Voicemail Message for Your Korean Professor
Individual Speaking

Student Name:

▶Include the following information in your voicemail message:

- Greeting
- Why you are calling
- Asking the professor whether he/she is available for a meeting
- Reasons why you want to meet
- Suggesting the date and time when you want to go to your professor's office
- Other suggestions/requests you would like to make of your professor
- Closing

NOTES

(1) Organize your voicemail message naturally.

(2) Use phone expressions as much as possible.

(3) Add more information if you have time.

Write a Postcard to Your Friend while Studying in Korea
Collaborative Speaking & Writing

Student Names: &

▶ **Include the following information in your postcard:**

- Description of Seoul and the weather there
- How you and your partner have been doing
- Four things that you and your partner have liked and disliked about studying in Korea
- Four things that you and your partner wish that you could have done but couldn't
- Four pieces of advice that you want to give about Korean culture to 스티브

NOTES

(1) Feel free to change the order of the information listed above.

(2) Organize your postcard coherently.

(3) Add more information if you have time.

Chapter 06
Task 2

Write a Postcard to a Friend You Met during Study Abroad in Korea
Individual Writing

Student Name:

▶ **Include the following information in your postcard:**
- Description of your life in the U.S.
- How you have been doing while staying in Korea
- Four things that you couldn't do while staying in Korea
- Two things that you want to do with 광수 in the U.S.
- Four pieces of advice, including at least two reasons

> **NOTES**
>
> (1) *Feel free to change the order of the information listed above.*
> (2) *Organize your postcard coherently.*
> (3) *Add more information if you have time.*

Send a Video Message to a Friend You Met during Study Abroad in Korea
Individual Speaking

Student Name:

▶ **Include the following information in your video message:**

- Greetings
- Description of your life in the U.S.
- Four things that you couldn't do while studying abroad in Korea
- Four things that you want to do with 광수 in the U.S.
- Four pieces of advice including at least two reasons
- Closing

(1) Feel free to change the order of the information listed above.

(2) Organize your video message coherently.

(3) Add more information if you have time.

Chapter 06
Task 4:
Real World Task

Send a Postcard to Your Friend

Individual Writing

Student Name:

▶ **Include the following information in your postcard:**

• Three things about how you have been doing recently

• The weather in the place that you visited

• Two fun activities you did there

• What you couldn't do while visiting there (at least three things)

• Four pieces of advice that you want to give your friend if they visit the place, including at least two reasons

NOTES

(1) Feel free to change the order of the information listed above.

(2) Organize your postcard coherently.

(3) Add more information if you have time.

Chapter 07
Task 1

Write a Shopping Blog Post

Collaborative Speaking & Writing

Student Names: &

▶ **Include the information below in your blog:**

- What you and your partner did while shopping and afterward
- 4 items that you and your partner bought
- How you and your partner are going to use the 4 items
- What you and your partner need to remember about the 4 items

---

NOTES

(1) Feel free to change the order of the information listed above.

(2) Organize your blog post coherently.

(3) Add more information if you have time (e.g., adding your own hashtags).

Shopping Blog

Fonts ▾ 15 ▾ **B** *I* U ꜀T ꜀T. Ⓣ | ☰ ꞮꞮ | ※ 𝒮

\# _____   \# _____

Shopping Blog

\# _____   \# _____

Shopping Blog

Fonts ⌄   15 ⌄   **B** *I* U̲ T̶ T. T̲ | ☰ ⊥ | ※ ⸜

\# _____   \# _____

Chapter 07
Task 2

Write a Blog Post for a Moving Sale

Individual Writing

Student Name:

▶ **Include the information below in your blog:**
• Background information about why you are selling an item
• Information about the item you want to sell (e.g., who would enjoy this item, good things about it, things to remember, the price, free item you can give away)
• Further information about your sale
• How people can get to your dormitory

NOTES

(1) Feel free to change the order of the information listed above.

(2) Organize your blog post coherently.

(3) Add more information if you have time (e.g., adding your own hashtags).

커피머신을 팔아요!

Fonts ⌄   15 ⌄   **B** *I* U̲ T̶ T. T̲ ☰ Ⲓ ※ 𝒮

\#_____ \#_____

커피머신을 팔아요!

Fonts ∨   15 ∨   **B**   *I*   U̲   T̶   T.   T̄ | ☰   ⊥ | ✕   𝒮

\#_____   \#_____

| 🖼 | ☁ | 🎥 | ☺ | 66 ˅ | — ˅ | ⊕ | 🔗 | ◉ | 🔍 | ▤ | 📅 | ▦ |

Fonts ˅   15 ˅   **B** *I* <u>U</u> T̅ T̲. [T] | ≡ ⊞ | ✳ 𝒮

기숙사까지 오는 길

도착해서 저한테 전화해 주세요.

_____

\# _____ \# _____

Chapter 07
Task 3

Create a Product Review Video on Your Shopping Blog
Individual Speaking

Student Name:

▶ **Include the following information in your product review video:**
- Greetings
- Personal introduction
- Description of two items
  - When and where you bought the items
  - Why you bought the items
- What you can do with the items
- Things that people need to remember when using the items
- To whom you will recommend the items
- Closing

NOTES

(1) Feel free to change the order of the information listed above.

(2) Organize your review video coherently.

(3) Add more information if you have time.

Create a Product Review Video on Your Shopping Blog

Individual Speaking

Student Name:

▶ **Include the following information in your product review video:**

• Personal introduction

• When and why you bought the item you chose

• How were you able to use the item and how it performed

• What you had to do after using the item

• At least two pros and cons of the item with reasons

• To whom you would recommend the item

NOTES

(1) Feel free to change the order of the information listed above.

(2) Organize your review video coherently.

(3) Add more information if you have time.

Make a Vlog Entry Comparing Korean Restaurants before Visiting
Collaborative Speaking

Student Names: &

▶ **Include the following information in your vlog entry:**

• Opening – ask whether your partner has tried any Korean restaurants

• Description of two restaurants in terms of the following information:

  - Location

  - Popular menu items

  - Pros and cons

• What you and your partner want to try at the restaurants

• Which restaurant you and your partner will go to together

• Closing

NOTES

(1) Feel free to change the order of the information listed above.

(2) Organize your vlog entry coherently.

(3) Add more information if you have time.

Student Name:

▶ **Include the following information in your vlog entry:**
- Greetings
- The purpose of the vlog entry
- The reason why you couldn't go with your partner
- Information about the restaurant and the food
  - What the restaurant was like
  - The dishes that you and your family ordered
  - What the foods you and your family ordered were like
  - What you and your family did
- Things that you tried
- Information about 중식당 that you and your partner want to visit
- Closing by recommending the restaurant to your viewers:
  "이렇게 저는 주말에 한식당에 가 봤는데요.
  _____기 때문에 좋았어요. 여러분도 한번 가 보세요."

NOTES

(1) Feel free to change the order of the information listed above.

(2) Organize your vlog entry coherently.

(3) Add more information if you have time.

Student Name:

▶ **Include the following information in your vlog entry script:**

• Greetings

• Two places where you want to go

• Two kinds of food that you want to try, including their characteristics and reasons why you want to try them

• Activities you want to try, including reasons why you want to try them

• Closing by asking the audience what they want to do in Korea and include the following sentence:
"제가 한국에 가서 해 드릴게요."

NOTES

(1) Feel free to change the order of the information listed above.

(2) Organize your vlog entry script coherently.

(3) Add more information if you have time.

Create a Vlog Entry about Your Favorite Places in Town

Individual Speaking

Student Name:

▶ **Include the following information in your vlog entry:**

• Greetings

• Introduction of places, foods, and activities

• Suggestions of places to go and reasons why

• Suggestions of foods to try and reasons why

• Suggestions of activities to try and reasons why

• Additional information about things to enjoy while visiting your neighborhood

• Closing

NOTES

(1) Feel free to change the order of the information listed above.

(2) Organize your vlog entry coherently.

(3) Add more information if you have time.